SPECIAL EDITION
2006

**By Mary Packard
and the Editors of Ripley Entertainment Inc.**

SCHOLASTIC INC.

New York   Toronto   London   Auckland   Sydney

Mexico City   New Delhi   Hong Kong   Buenos Aires

Library of Congress Cataloging-in-Publication Data

Packard, Mary.

Ripley's Believe It or Not! / by Mary Packard and the editors of Ripley Entertainment Inc.—Special ed.

2006

p. cm.

ISBN 0-439-71830-9

1. Curiosities and wonders—Juvenile literature. I. Ripley Entertainment Inc. II. Title.

AG243.P24 2005

031.02—dc22   2004025040

Developed by Nancy Hall, Inc.

Edited by Linda Falken

Designed by Atif Toor and Iram Khandwala

Cover design by Louise Bova

Photo research by Sharon Lennon

12 11 10 9 8 7 6 5 4 3 2 1   5 6 7 8 9 10/0

Printed in China

First printing, September 2005

CONTENTS

WIZARD OF ODDS

THE BABY THAT WAS BLOWN 70 FEET BY GUNPOWDER - AND LIVED!
AN INFANT SLEEPING IN ITS CRADLE ON GREAT TOWER ST, LONDON, ENGLAND, WAS HURTLED TO THE ROOF OF A NEARBY CHURCH BY AN EXPLOSION THAT DEMOLISHED ITS HOME -YET THE BABY WAS FOUND SLUMBERING PEACEFULLY IN ITS UNDAMAGED CRADLE!
THE CHILD'S PARENTS WERE AMONG THOSE KILLED ITS IDENTITY WAS NEVER DISCOVERED (Jan...

THE STRANGEST DRAMATIC SCHOOL IN HISTORY
CHARLES DULLIN (1885-1949) the brilliant French actor RECEIVED HIS DRAMATIC TRAINING RECITING POETRY DAILY FOR SEVERAL YEARS IN A CAGE FULL OF LIONS

Hold onto your hat. You're about to enter the weird and wacky world of Ripley's Believe It or Not! It's a fantastical world created by Robert Ripley, a self-taught artist who turned his love of the bizarre into a hugely successful empire. His massive collection of incredible facts is continually being updated and expanded by teams of Ripley researchers around the world. So get ready to experience the world as you've never experienced it before—a world that includes two-faced kittens, skydiving dogs, people trying to look like animals, camera-covered vans, and much, much more. The world is weirder than you think.

Believe It!®

Mexican artist Enrico Angelis Ramos paints on dead animals, such as bats!

F R E A K

Eric Sprague, also known as Lizardman, is doing his best to look like his favorite reptiles. Besides being tattooed from head to toe with scales, he's had his teeth sharpened, his tongue split, and a horny ridge implanted in his forehead!

Harrod Blank's camera van has more than 2,000 cameras attached to it, all operated by shutter buttons on the dashboard!

Travelin' Man

As his fame grew, Robert Ripley roamed the corners of the world in search of the unbelievable. On one trip alone, he crossed two continents, covering 24,000 miles—10,000 of them by donkey, horse, and camel. Throughout his travels, Ripley was always on the lookout for weird treasures—and he found more than he bargained for! Whether in the jungles of Papua New Guinea, on the Great Wall of China, or halfway up an Egyptian pyramid, he always came away with new and awesome wonders to add to his collections.

MAN OF MANY FIRSTS

Robert Ripley was the first person to broadcast to every nation in the world, the first millionaire cartoonist in history, and the first syndicated columnist to receive more than a million letters per year.

Get ready to take two Ripley Road Trips! On one, you will relive Robert Ripley's real-life adventures in China (page 18). On the other, you will travel across America (page 110) for a firsthand look at its most outrageous structures.

Shrunken heads and ancestor skulls are a few of Ripley's more grotesque souvenirs.

At the Paco Cemetery in the Philippines, loved ones pay an annual rental fee to lay their dead to rest in chambers in the cemetery's wall. On a visit in 1932, Robert Ripley stopped by to inspect the graves.

The Funky First-Aid timeline (page 26) lets you experience firsthand how the science of medicine has evolved through the ages, while The Remains of the Day timeline (page 90) takes you on a tour of mummies around the world.

1

ODD-YSSEY

Camel-lots!

Every October or November, thousands of camels converge on Pushkar, India, for the Camel Fair. Decked out in brilliantly colored textiles, the camels parade their finery and compete in races. Then, to the amazement of onlookers, the animals dance and perform acrobatics! They even compete in contests to determine the best-decorated camel and the best camel haircut. What better way to honor an animal that has transported its citizens across the deserts for centuries?

SQUIRRELLY!

Olney, Illinois, is so proud of its colony of rare albino squirrels that the police wear badges engraved with a squirrel and ticket anyone who bothers the pure white animals.

Greasing the Way

In ancient Japan, warriors smeared toad grease on themselves in the belief it would make them puncture-proof. Since the warriors fought with swords and daggers, a lot of toads had to be pulverized to protect them. To comfort the souls of all those dead toads, the Japanese hold the Mount Tsukuba Toad Festival each year on the first Sunday in August. At the festival, vendors sell small containers of toad grease to be used on cuts. Giant models of toads are even paraded through the grounds of the Mount Tsukuba Shinto Shrine—which is itself toad-shaped!

Shock Treatment

In October 2003, a 220-pound Asiatic black bear walked through the main entrance of a hospital in Ichinoseki, Japan. Screams startled the bear, which turned around and crashed through an emergency exit. The bear then came and left again, taking exactly the same route, before escaping back into the nearby mountains.

RIPLEY FILE: 1.12.64

Horsing around! For centuries, a grueling cross-country race has been staged during the annual Naadam Festival in Mongolia in order to determine the country's fastest horses. Hundreds of horses compete in a mad dash over an 18-mile-long course—all of them ridden by children ages five to thirteen! Why? Lightweight riders allow the horses to run faster.

SMALL WORLD

Floating on Air

Each year in late May, the island of Cheung Chau, near Hong Kong, holds the Bun Festival, which dates back to the 1600s. On the last day of the festival, thousands of warm, freshly baked buns are attached to three 52.5-foot-tall towers in front of the Pak Tai Temple to appease the restless spirits of the dead. Then comes a spectacular parade of colorfully costumed children who seem to float in the air. The children are secured with invisible wires, but for spectators, the illusion is magical.

KEEPING CURRENT

In remote places unreachable by roads, such as along the banks of the Orinoco River in Venezuela, library boats filled with books help people keep up with their reading.

Blessed Event

In January 2004, 83-year-old Pope John Paul II attended a break-dancing performance at Vatican City. Music blared from a boom box as various dancers performed tricky acrobatic moves, including leaps, twists, and flips. One performer stood on his head and spun like a top, winning applause from the Pope and other Vatican officials.

Daredevils

Since 1620, the town of Castrillo de Murcia in Spain has celebrated the Catholic religious holiday of Corpus Christi in a most unusual way—with a baby-jumping festival! During the festival, a man called *El Colacho* (the tailed one), who represents the devil, dresses up in a yellow and red costume and leaps over babies born in the previous year. Why? It's said that as *El Colacho* jumps, he takes evil with him, leaving the infants cleansed of original sin.

WACKY!

Loo With a View

There's a new way to view London, thanks to artist Monica Bonvicini. She has created a one-way mirrored public toilet outside of the Tate Britain gallery. Someone inside the toilet, or "loo" (as they say in England), can see outside, but passersby can't see in.

Art-Warming

Viewers warm to the art of Canadian artist Janet Morton. Morton took to using yarn in her art in 1992 and has since decked out such unlikely things as animals, trees, and houses in her hand-knit creations. For one project, she knitted a sweater for a giraffe, a cap for a rhinoceros, and socks for an elephant in the Toronto Zoo. In another project, Morton dressed a house for winter, covering it with a "cozy" made from more than 800 recycled sweaters. She also knit warm garments for a TV, a chair, tables—and even a plant!

Wheel-ly Silly!

Competitors streak toward the finish line of the Outhouse Race on Old Timers Day in Hagerman, New Mexico. Each spring, contestants mount outhouses on wheels and race them through the streets.

RIPLEY FILE: 8.27.61

Timely additions!

For 400 years, a single male mechanical figure sounded the bell of the ornate clock on the church of Notre Dame in Dijon, France. That is until 1610, when the city council commissioned a wife to be built for him. In 1714, a son was added and in 1881, a daughter.

TOILET TRAINING

A town in Brazil has found a way to keep its beach clean—toilets for dogs! Each one features a wood pole for liquid waste and a bin for solid waste. Now if only dogs could read!

DAFFY DOINGS

What a Crab!

Every August for more than 30 years, Ocean City, New Jersey, has hosted the Miss Crustacean Hermit Crab Beauty Contest. About 50 proud owners decorate their crabs' shells to compete for the tasty Cucumber Rind Cup. Past entrants have included crabs dressed up as skiers (left), surfers, a hermit crab basketball team, and single entries such as Cleopatra Crab and King Crablantis—yes, despite the competition's title, both male and female crabs can compete.

Having a Ball

Imagine being tossed around inside a giant beach ball as it rolls down a hill. That's kind of how "Zorbonauts" feel—folks who are trying out the new sport called "Zorbing." Invented in New Zealand, the Zorb is made up of one big, spongy, clear plastic ball inside another. The two balls are separated by about two feet of space inflated with air. To reach the inner ball, you crawl through a tube, which also lets in fresh air. Then the Zorb is rolled down a hill. Inside, you can turn somersaults, run backward, strap yourself in, add a bit of water to the inside so you slide around— whatever seems like the most fun!

CREATING A FLAP

In 1991, a stranger flew into New York City. The newcomer made his home on one of New York's most prestigious blocks along Central Park West. In fact, Mary Tyler Moore shares his building, which is just across the street from Woody Allen's. Who is this stranger? He's a red-tailed hawk, the first ever to live in modern-day Manhattan.

Dubbed Pale Male because of his cream-colored chest feathers, the hawk became an instant celebrity, attracting a crowd every day of the week. Bird lovers—millionaires and homeless alike—are so enthralled with the feathered city slicker that they often arrive at the crack of dawn to watch him and stay until dusk. A 97-year-old retired dentist watches the bird from his next-door apartment. One high-tech bird-watcher keeps an eye on Pale Male with sophisticated camera equipment and TV monitors. Pale Male even stars in his own documentary produced by Fredric Lilian, who spent six years filming the famous bird and his brood.

In 1993, Pale Male's fans were treated to the spectacle of a female hawk preening her tail feathers right beside Pale Male on his 12th-story ledge. Dubbed First Love, she was Pale Male's first mate. Since then, Pale Male has had three mates and fathered more than 20 baby hawks. Whenever there are eggs in the nest, the number of observers swells. As each new fledgling perches on the ledge of the 12-story apartment building and begins to flap its wings, the crowd is so quiet, you can hear a pin drop. That all changes as soon as it's clear the bird has successfully made its first flight, and the crowd erupts in cheers.

In December 2004, Pale Male's nest was torn down, but loyal neighbors and friends came out in droves and rallied to have it rebuilt.

PUCKER UP!

In China, the coolest way to say "I love you" on Valentine's Day is to present your loved one with a pair of kissing fish, also called gouramis. Hopefully, the fish will last longer than flowers or chocolates!

KAZAKHSTAN

MONGOLIA

1: X'ian In 1974, workers digging a well accidentally discovered the tomb of Qin Shi Huangdi (259–210 B.C.E.), who unified China and became its first emperor. Archaeologists were astounded to find the tomb guarded by a terra-cotta army of more than 8,000 life-size warriors, including cavalrymen on horseback and in horse-drawn chariots. Even more amazing is that no two soldiers' faces are alike. Each has his own distinct features and expression, from smiling to looking downright ferocious.

CHINA

PAKISTAN

① ② ④

2: Chongqing

Robert Ripley met the enterprising man shown in this wax replica in 1923. In need of a way to earn money, the so-called "Lighthouse Man" drilled a hole in his head and plugged it with a candle to light the way for visitors through the dark streets of his city.

INDIA

MYANMAR (BURMA)

LAOS

3: Fuzhou

In 1946, Robert Ripley bought his beloved *Mon Lei*, an authentic junk built in the 1780s to haul fish along the Fuzhou River. Ripley painted the engine with eyes, claws, and whiskers to honor the ancient Chinese belief that boats were fast because a dragon lived inside them. He also painted this watercolor of the *Mon Lei*.

4: Sichuan Province

Most of the roughly 1,000 giant pandas left in the wild live in Sichuan. Thanks to places like the Wolong Nature Preserve, these rare animals may soon have a better chance of surviving. One factor that contributes to their rarity is a low birthrate. At Wolong, scientists study artificial breeding in the hope that more pandas can be born in captivity and later be released in the wild. Newborn pandas weigh just three to five ounces. They are so small they can be held in their mother's mouth!

5: Xiamen

A temple dedicated to the god of bridges and roads stands on a span across the Jiulong River, near Xiamen, so travelers can conveniently pray for a safe journey.

RUSSIA

EAST CHINA SEA

JAPAN

3

5

TAIWAN

VIETNAM

SOUTH CHINA SEA

MACAO

EXTRA! EXTRA!

On the Hook

In June 2004, fisherman Robert Davies of Llanelli, Wales, accidentally netted a 264-pound sturgeon. Sturgeon is rarely caught in British waters and is the source of caviar, a costly delicacy. That's why it's on a list of "royal fish" and must be offered first to the queen. Davies did so and received permission to "dispose of it as he saw fit." However, when he sold the fish, it was seized by wildlife officers because it's illegal to sell sturgeon, which is a protected species. If convicted, Davies could face six months in prison or a fine of more than $9,000. Let's hope he'll be let off the hook!

Cover-up

In May 2004, indignant neighbors of ex-army Sergeant Tony Watson of Barsley, England, reported him to police for indecent exposure. When police arrived, Watson was fully clothed—but his garden gnomes were not. Watson was let off with a warning, but to avoid future police visits, he provided his gnomes with painted-on swimwear.

Barfburg

Kotzen means "puke" in German, which is why a number of citizens in Kotzen, Germany, were lobbying for a name change. Unfortunately, however, they couldn't agree on an alternative, so when it came time for officials to vote, the name change was vetoed by a vote of five to three. Not all the citizens were sorry, though—the name of their town never fails to make newcomers smile!

City of the Gods

There are 863 temples built for the gods alone on the holy mountain of Satrunjaya in India. The temples close at dusk and no visitors, including priests, may stay past sunset.

Pizza Police

In an effort to clamp down on "pizza pirates"—people in Italy who sell substandard pies and call them "pizza"—inspectors have been hired by the Italian government to make sure restaurant owners comply with new pizza rules. The guidelines dictate everything about a pizza from the thickness of its crust to the temperature at which it should be cooked. The punishment for those who fail to comply has yet to be determined.

Scared to Death

Chickens belonging to a farmer in Huxian, China, had an extreme reaction to a police siren that went off just a little more than ten yards away. Thirty-five of the chickens dropped dead seconds after the siren went off, and the remaining 400 died shortly thereafter from shock. The farmer is suing police for scaring his chickens to death.

Long-Term Parking

A South African woman accidentally deposited a rare gold coin worth more than a $1,000 in a parking meter in Paarl (outside Capetown) while shopping without her glasses!

Gas Tax

In New Zealand, about 90 percent of the methane emissions that contribute to global warming are produced by livestock. To fund further research, the government decided to place a flatulence tax on cows and sheep. However, due to protests from angry farmers, the plans were dumped.

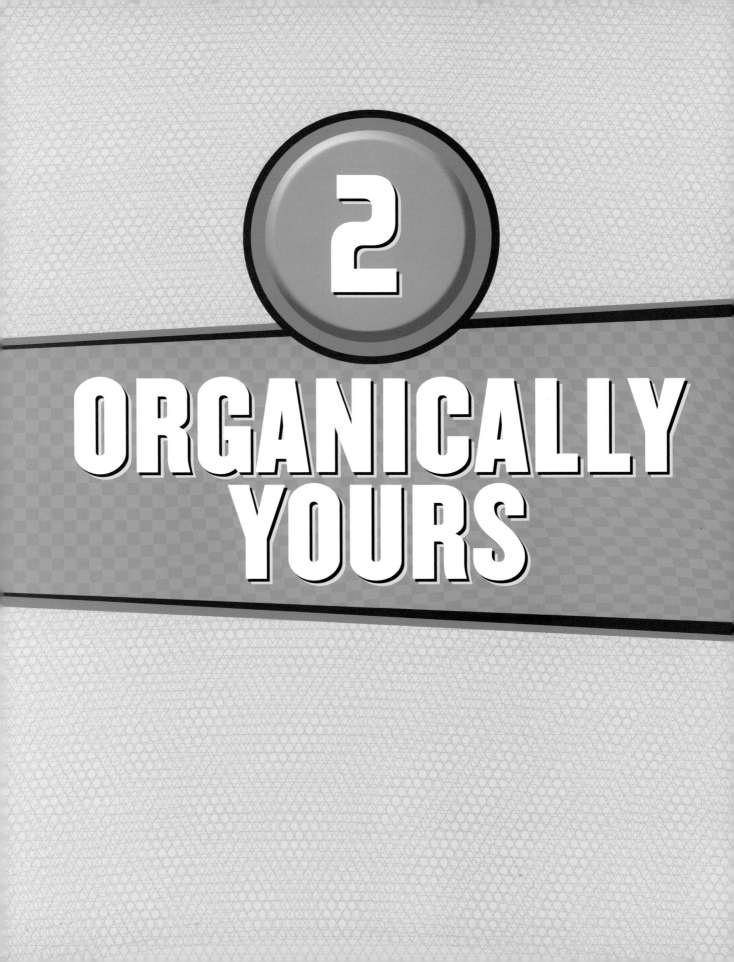

2

ORGANICALLY YOURS

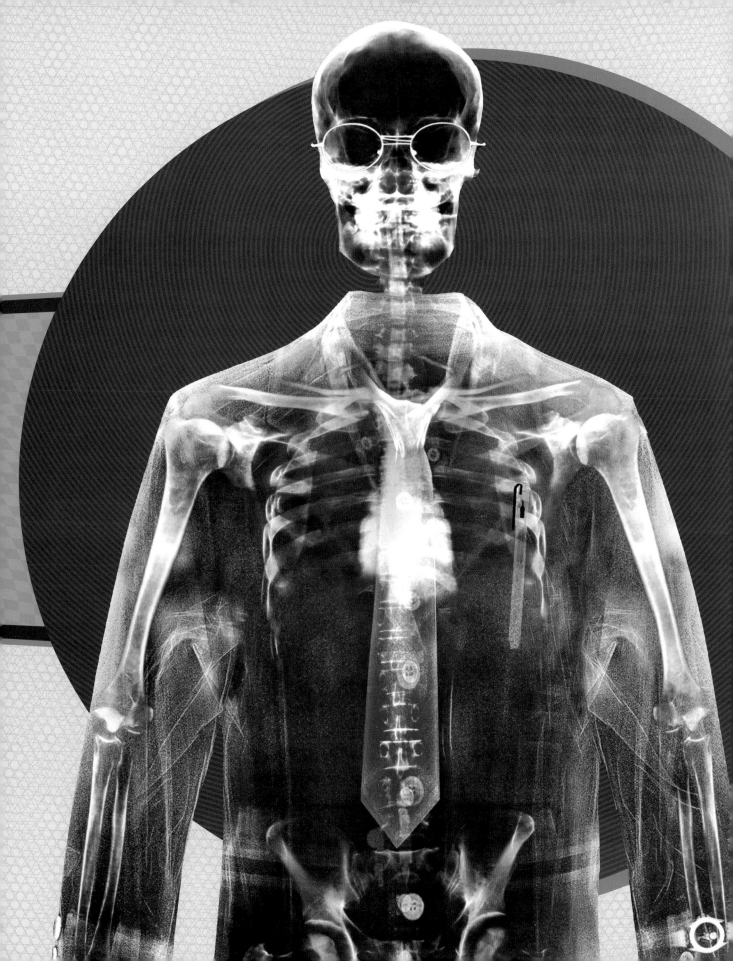

UP CLOSE

Got Bugs?

There are millions of bacteria living inside your intestines. Bacteria are live organisms that feed on the food you eat and help break it down for digestion. What's leftover is gas. A lot of it is absorbed by the intestinal walls. What isn't is released through the mouth in the form of burps—or in another, more embarrassing, way!

SWEATING IT OUT

What does sweat have in common with urine? Both are made up of the same chemicals, only in different proportions.

The Inside Scoop

Grossology is the name of an interactive exhibit where kids can learn about the human body. Young visitors to museums, science centers, or schools hosting Grossology get to play "gas attack pinball," climb a wart-and-pimple-covered wall, and pass through a 30-foot-long, 3-D model of the digestive system. Who would have guessed learning could be so . . . gross?

Gas man! Paul Hunn of Great Britain has the world's loudest belch—118.1 decibels, which is equal in intensity to the sound of an airplane taking off!

Tiny Terrors

Tiny organisms called scabies mites can burrow beneath your skin and set up house there. Related to the spider family, scabies mites are parasites. That means they feast on you. When they do, they cause a fearsome itch. They leave short, wavy, red tracks on the skin that end in a blister. The blister is where the female has laid her eggs. Scratch the blister and you'll be sorry. When the blister pops, out come more mites to make the itch even worse!

FUNKY FIRST-AID

37995 B.C.E.

Archaeologists have unearthed skulls dating back as far as 40,000 years ago with holes drilled into them. The holes are evidence of trepanning, which is considered the oldest form of brain surgery.

1100s C.E.

In Europe, ground-up ancient Egyptian mummy skin and wrappings was used to treat skin rashes and upset stomachs.

1799

Bloodletting, the practice of cutting open a vein to release blood, was once used to treat just about every manner of illness. To help George Washington (1732–1799) recover from a very bad cold, his veins were bled extensively, removing about half the blood in his body, a treatment many believe was the cause of his death later that same day.

1816

When an overweight woman showed up at the office of Dr. René Théophile-Hyacinthe Laënnec (1781–1826) in Paris, France, he couldn't feel her heartbeat through all the fat. Nor did he consider it proper to lay his ear to a woman's chest. Laënnec thought for a minute, then rolled 24 sheets of paper into a cylinder, placed it to the woman's chest, and—voilà!—he could hear her heart perfectly. Laënnec had created the world's first stethoscope!

2000

Deoxyribonucleic acid (DNA) is the molecule that contains our genes, the parts of cells that make us who we are. In 2000, scientists managed to string together all three billion rungs of the DNA ladder in the correct order. Now they plan to learn the function of each gene. When they do, they'll have a complete map of what makes humans tick.

1500s

In Great Britain and Europe, barbers once doubled as surgeons. Maybe that's because they had the sharpest scissors and knives, which were not only good for cutting hair but also for lancing boils, amputating limbs, and performing oral surgery!

1700s

In Europe, watching surgery was a major form of entertainment. Surgeons would actually invite their friends to watch them operate. That's why operating rooms are also called theaters!

2001

Believe It or Not! Surgeons in New York successfully removed the gall bladder of a woman in a hospital in France. With the aid of a video camera and a high-speed fiber-optic line, the surgeons manipulated the arm of a surgical robot to perform the operation.

GRAY MATTERS

Monkey Think, Monkey Do

Scientists, led by Miguel Nicolelis at Duke University, hope that people who are paralyzed will one day benefit from experiments conducted with monkeys in 2003. After implanting tiny electrodes in two monkeys' brains, the scientists ran wires from the electrodes to a robotic arm in another room. Then they taught the monkeys how to use a joystick to make the robotic arm reach and grasp objects. As soon as the monkeys mastered the joystick, the researchers unplugged it. Amazingly, the monkeys continued to control the robotic arm—by their thoughts alone! Now, similar tests are being conducted with quadriplegics, people who have no movement below their neck.

Buzz Cut

In 1990, airplane mechanic Ivan Schlutz of Longmont, Colorado, was working on an engine when it turned over, setting the propeller in motion. The propeller hit Schlutz on the top of the head, damaging 40 percent of his skull and sending the bone slicing into his brain. Amazingly, Schlutz recovered and, while in rehabilitation, he began modeling clay. Soon, he was taking classes and creating beautiful bronze sculptures. His doctors think that since the practical left side of his brain was most seriously damaged, the creative right side had to take over. Schlutz isn't complaining. His masterpieces fetch upward of $5,000 apiece.

CAT SCANS

With the use of brain-imaging devices such as CAT scans, researchers can actually see inside the brain and observe how it works. Before these tools were available, however, doctors could do little more than guess at what caused abnormal human behavior—which is why a myth about the mental health of a British artist was born.

Louis Wain (1860–1939) was famous for his fanciful drawings and paintings of cats (right). At the height of his popularity, his art appeared in calendars, greeting cards, books and magazines, and on the walls of schoolrooms all over England. In 1923, Wain was confined to an insane asylum. Doctors did not know the cause of Wain's mental illness, but it did not stop him from continuing to paint until his death.

In the late 1930s, a psychiatrist named Walter Maclay bought eight of Wain's more abstract paintings (below) in a London shop. Maclay arranged the paintings in the order he thought they'd been painted. In the 1950s, these paintings became the basis for a theory stating that Wain suffered from schizophrenia and that his paintings grew more abstract as his disease progressed. Fascinating though the theory was, there was no basis for it in fact. Wain was never diagnosed with schizophrenia, and since the eight paintings were not dated, there was no way to tell if they had been painted while he was sick. Nevertheless, the myth caught on—and can still be found in college textbooks today!

HOW PUZZLING!

I See Right Through You!

Natalya Demkina of Saransk, Russia, was talking at six months old and reading by the age of three. However, that's nothing compared to what she could do at age sixteen. Demkina claims she can switch from normal vision to X-ray vision. Though doctors at Saransk Children's Hospital administered exhaustive tests in January 2004, they remain baffled by Demkina's detailed and accurate descriptions of what she sees inside human bodies—including previously undetected illnesses.

WEIGHED DOWN

In 2004, surgeons operated on 50-year-old Mangilal Jain of India and found 728 kidney stones inside his body—more than four times the previous record!

Phony Feelings!

In 1998, Matthew Botvinick, then of the University Health Center of Pittsburgh, Pennsylvania, conducted an experiment in tactile ventriloquism—when someone feels sensations in something that is not a part of his or her body. Botvinick had people sit at a table with one arm placed behind a screen where it couldn't be seen. Then he set a fake rubber hand on the table with one end touching the person's body. Using brushes to tickle the real hand and the rubber hand at the same time, he found that at least once during the experiment, every person tested said that he or she could feel the brush stroking the fake hand!

RIPLEY FILE:
12.29.66

Baby-sitting! Jack Jones, son of Mr. and Mrs. James Jones of Rockford, Illinois, could sit up unassisted just one week after his birth!

Good News!

After years of taking a bad rap, chocolate is no longer a no-no. In one study, chemicals in dark chocolate were shown to lower blood pressure. Another study found that those same chemicals could fight cancer, too. *Yum, yum!*

What a Flake!

Reptiles are not the only animals that shed their skin. Take a look at your own skin. What you see is dead. You'll soon lose it all, flake by flake. In fact, humans lose billions of skin cells every day. Fortunately, there is new skin beneath the dead cells. Consider this: The expensive creams sold in stores are meant to be smeared over skin that is already dead!

Dung Gum

The president of Turkmenistan has issued a decree banning *nas*, a popular chewed energy booster, which—Believe It or Not!— contains chicken excrement.

Ouch!

During the 1500s, gunshot wounds were treated by pouring hot oil on them. The scalding stopped the bleeding, but the pain was unbearable. In 1537, Ambroise Paré (1517–1590) ran out of oil while treating wounded soldiers on the battlefield, so he mixed up an ointment of egg yolks, turpentine, and oil of roses. To his surprise, the ointment worked. From then on, Paré led the way in humane treatments and eventually became known as the "father of modern surgery."

Tooth Wizards

Dentists in medieval England, who were known as "tooth drawers," wore pointed caps and necklaces made from extracted teeth!

Five Dead Mice

What do some people in China do with an elixir called Mice Saki? They drink it to cure colds, improve circulation, and to strengthen the lower back. They rub it on their skin to get rid of aches and pains, as well. If five individual mice are not visible floating around in your bottle of Mice Saki, the manufacturer guarantees that your money will be returned.

Smelly Reaction

In 2003, scientists at the University of Parma, Italy, hooked up research subjects to Magnetic Resonance Imaging machines (MRIs) and had them watch a film of people reacting to disgusting, pleasant, and neutral odors. Then they had the subjects smell all the same things themselves. To the scientists' surprise, the subjects' brains showed the same pattern of activity no matter whether they simply observed someone else's emotional reaction or actually experienced it themselves.

Slick Trick

Researchers at Northwestern University in Illinois have developed a blood substitute similar to Teflon, a nonstick cookware coating.

Gulp!

Each year, about 250,000 people travel to Hyderabad, India, at the beginning of the monsoon season to receive a cure for asthma given out for free by the Gouda family. Each person gulps down a wriggly three-inch-long fish stuffed with a secret herbal formula that has been in the family since 1845. People who've taken the cure claim that they feel better. Others, including doctors, think the cure is more than a little fishy!

Red Alert

Believe It or Not! Whenever you blush, the lining of your stomach becomes redder!

3

WHAT IN THE WORLD?

PLANT-ZILLA!

BAD SEED

The rosary pea has beautiful, bright red seeds with a black spot on one end, which are sometimes used as beads. The seeds, however, are so poisonous that eating just one can be fatal!

Scent-sational!

In July 2004, botanists at the University of Connecticut were delighted when their Titan arum plant bloomed for the first time in ten years. Also known as the corpse flower, the Titan arum of Indonesia can live as long as 40 years but only blooms two or three times. Its bloom, however, is among the largest in the world. When mature, the tall central shoot heats up, producing a smell like rotting flesh. In the wild, the plants grow few and far between, and the stench attracts flies, which will carry the pollen from plant to plant.

Phony ID

The markings on the flowers, stems, or pods of certain plants make them look a lot like aphids, caterpillars, or other bugs. Why? To keep animals and other insects from dining on them. Other plants go on the offensive. For example, sundew plants have tentacles that glisten in the sun, making them look wet with dew. The sticky fluid attracts and traps insects. Then the tentacles slowly close over the hapless bug, while digestive enzymes in the fluid break down its body into food the plant can absorb.

RIPLEY FILE:
10.12.67

Way to grow! The rope trees on Bega in the Fiji Islands grow trunks that wind and twist horizontally and can often grow to 500 feet in length.

The Banyan Strangler

Indian banyan trees can be 100 feet tall, have thousands of supporting trunks, and cover several acres. Yet their survival depends on a single type of wasp for pollination and birds to carry their seeds to other trees. After a banyan seed is deposited on a branch, it sprouts aerial roots, which absorb nutrients from the air. Once the roots touch the ground, however, they take hold and grow into supporting trunks. Eventually, the banyan strangles its host tree. The largest Indian banyan is said to grow near Poona, India, and measure a half-mile around!

FUEL FOR THOUGHT

Warm Leavings

How does Tierpark Hellabrunn Zoo in Munich, Germany, plan to generate heat? It will fuel its own buildings with a biomass power plant that converts such things as grass cuttings, food leftovers, and dung into fuel. With huge animals such as elephants and rhinos living at the zoo, the droppings should be more than enough to do the job!

FRUITY!

Researchers in Australia hope to harness the methane gas produced by the bacteria that munch on tons of rotting bananas to produce enough electricity to light up 500 homes!

Garbage In . . .

Now garbage, such as used tires, plastics, raw sewage, and even your Thanksgiving leftovers, doesn't have to go to . . . well, waste. Changing World Technologies is the first company to commercially use thermal processing—placing materials under pressure and heating them up—to convert organic waste into clean fuel.

SPEECH BUBBLE: FILL IT UP WITH PREMIUM! AIR

Full of hot air! Inventor Guy Negre has developed a car that runs on compressed air and can reach speeds of 70 miles per hour!

Tree-mendous!

One ton of recycled paper saves 12 trees, up to 24,000 gallons of water, and 41,000 kilowatt hours of energy—enough to provide a house with energy for six months!

BOTTLE LABELS: Raw Oil Product · Refined Oil (Swine Manure) · Solid product (char + inert)

Crude!

It costs pig farmers a lot of money to get rid of pig manure—but that may change in the future. If researchers at the University of Illinois in Urbana have their way, pig manure will one day be used in specially built home furnaces that can turn the manure into crude oil! Best of all, instead of paying to dispose of hog waste, farmers would be able to sell it!

SECOND TIME AROUND

Cluck, Cluck!

Scientists working for the United States Department of Agriculture have developed a method of converting millions of pounds of chicken feathers into fiber. Then they use the fiber to make paper diapers, clothing, and insulation.

HOOKED ON BAGS!

Saroj Welch of Louisiana crochets plastic grocery bags into purses, sells them, and donates the proceeds to charity.

Twisted!

It took Frank Polifka 15 years to perfect the Windhexe, a machine that can pulverize almost anything tossed into it. Heated compressed air is forced through the top of an eight-foot-tall funnel-shaped can. Inside, the air spins around like a tornado, quickly turning anything from animal carcasses to concrete into a dry, sterile powder. The Windhexe may one day prove to be a clean, economical way to dispose of industrial waste. It might also be used to powder chicken byproducts for use in pet food and to separate collagen from eggshells for use in cosmetics and skin grafts.

Corn-tastic!

Plastic containers are pretty convenient. You can use them to carry your lunch or to store leftovers in. Too bad plastic is made from oil—a natural resource that is getting harder and harder to come by. Worse still, it takes centuries for plastic containers to decompose, making them very bad for the environment. Now Cargill Dow has a new product that is just the opposite. "Corntainers" are made from NatureWorks PLA, which is derived from corn, an annually renewable resource. Not only do "corntainers" save oil—they are 100 percent biodegradable!

Trash Couture

A fashion show sponsored by the Pennsylvania Department of Environmental Protection? You bet! On April 22, 1999, a show called "Recycled on the Runway" made its debut in Philadelphia before traveling to five other areas around the state. Models strutted down the runway wearing outfits that student designers created from recycled materials, such as Bubble Wrap, shredded microfilm, used zippers, and candy wrappers—all in an effort to educate the public about buying recycled products.

WACKY WEATHER

Slimed!

On two different days in June 2002, the residents of Sangrampur, India, panicked when a mysterious green rain fell on their town. They were extremely relieved when the West Bengal Pollution Control Board informed them that the green rain did not contain toxic chemicals. Instead, it was a mixture of pollen and the feces of a huge swarm of Asian honeybees flying overhead!

RIPLEY FILE: 11.20.60

Double Sun-days! Changes in the atmosphere made it appear as though there were two suns in the sky above the Scottish countryside near the river Spey for several days before the Great Storm of 1829.

Goal!

During a summer thunderstorm in 2003, a hailstone roughly the size of a soccer ball came crashing out of the sky in Aurora, Nebraska. Measuring seven inches in diameter, it left a crater 14 inches wide and 11 inches deep and holds the record for the largest hailstone ever to fall in the United States.

Wicked!

Run indoors, go to the basement, and stay away from doors and windows. That's what everyone who lives in the Great Plains section of the United States known as Tornado Alley does when a twister is coming—and even that doesn't always help. A tornado is dangerous enough on its own, but when a tornado outbreak hits, it can be devastating. The worst outbreak on record for the 20th century occurred during just 16 hours in April 1974, when a total of 148 tornadoes struck across 13 states, killing 315 people and injuring more than 5,000.

WHEN FISH FLY

In 2002, children in Lincoln County, Maine, were on their way to school when they were surprised by a downpour of flying fish pelting the windows of their school bus.

EXTRA! EXTRA!

Sweet Ride?

In 1996, a Michigan State University graduate student discovered that chocolate is a "smart fluid." What does that mean? When melted chocolate is zapped with an electrical charge, it becomes thick and gel-like. When the power's off, it goes back to being liquid. Car manufacturers are experimenting with using "smart fluids" in computer-controlled shock absorbers for a smoother ride. Does that mean your car will one day have chocolate shock absorbers? Probably not. Apparently if the voltage gets too high, the chocolate solidifies.

Bright Idea

Andrea Burke of Portland, Oregon, lives in a house made from recycled newspapers, ryegrass straw, and fluorescent lightbulbs. It was built for her in 1993 by the Sustainable Building Collaborative as a part of a conservationist program.

Shoe-ins

In 1991, Julie Lewis founded a company called Deja Shoe in Lake Oswego, Oregon, which introduced the first shoes ever made from recycled disposable diaper plastic, tires, paper bags, coffee filters, soda bottles, polystyrene cups, and corrugated cardboard. Decorations adorned the insides of the shoeboxes, so they could be turned inside out to make gift boxes. The company even donated a percentage of its profits to such worthy causes as Amnesty International and the Save Our Wild Salmon Coalition.

Abracadabra!

Each rainy season, a spring in Le Chatelet, France, dries up and disappears. Then in times of drought, the spring suddenly fills up with water and flows again.

Eeew!

In the 1880s, a fly deposited eggs in a Kansas man's nose while he slept. Not long after, the unthinkable happened. The eggs—250 of them—hatched in his nose! Attempts to remove the eggs surgically were unsuccessful. Sadly, the patient died after the maggots invaded other parts of his skull.

What a Waste!

Believe It or Not! The Pentagon produces more than a ton of toxic waste every minute!

Airheads

In 1991, sidewalk vendors in Mexico City began selling pure oxygen at a cost of 5,000 pesos—roughly $439—per minute to help counteract the effects of smog.

Stuff It!

Home furnishings designer Gaston Marticorena of New York City makes chairs that are as comfortable as they are unusual. Consider his round plastic bubble chairs that only take shape when you sit in them. Or his clear vinyl chairs stuffed with shredded income tax receipts. If you need a portable chair, try Marticorena's indoor-outdoor, fabric-covered inner-tube chair. To inflate it, simply get out your bicycle pump.

Perfect Storm!

In January 2000, a cottage in Malagash Point, Nova Scotia, Canada, was lifted from its foundation and set down a quarter mile away during a fierce winter storm. Believe It or Not!, everything inside remained intact, including the bottles sitting on top of the kitchen cabinets!

CUTTING EDGE

Eye-deal

You've seen earrings, nose rings, and even eyebrow rings, but now there's a new trend taking Rotterdam, the Netherlands, by storm: eyeball jewelry. The jewels are surgically implanted in the outer membrane of the front of the eyeball, giving new meaning to the phrase "sparkling eyes."

BEAUTY HURTS

It was once fashionable for young Inuit girls to tattoo their faces. To achieve the desired effect, they poked holes in their skin and pulled wet animal tendons blackened with carbon through them.

Ouch!

In March 2004, 18-year-old Robert Forster went to Stainless Studios in Las Cruces, New Mexico, for a piercing session. In less than two hours, Forster had had 1,400 needles inserted into his body—300 in his arms and 1,100 in his legs—setting a new world record.

RIPLEY FILE: 12.18.60

Had a very shiny nose! Danish astronomer Tycho Brahe (1546–1601) had his nose sliced off in a duel. He replaced it with a nose made of gold, silver, and wax that he wore for the rest of his life.

That's a Stretch!

Joanna Vaughn was born with dwarfism. She was too short to reach things on counters or shelves, and her arms were so short, she couldn't tie her shoelaces. When still in high school, Vaughn heard about a procedure being performed at the Cedars-Sinai Medical Center in Los Angeles, California, that could add inches to arms and legs. As soon as she graduated in 1994, Vaughn had her first operation. First, the bones of her lower legs were broken and external rods were attached. Then, every day, Vaughn or someone in her family turned adjusters, separating the bone bit by bit so new bone would grow in to fill the gap. Five years later, after undergoing the same procedure for her thighs and upper arms, Vaughn had gained almost 12 inches in her legs and four inches in her arms. Now at just about five feet tall, she can drive a car without pedal extensions—and even put her hands in her pockets.

BODIES OF CULTURE

Culture Vulture

Dr. Oldoinyo Laetoli Le Baaba of Los Angeles, California, was first introduced to Eastern cultures at the age of fourteen. As he learned about different societies, Le Baaba began to adopt some of their practices. After 20 years of changing his physical appearance, he has facial tattoos like those of the Maori tribes (bottom left) and ear piercings that mimic those of the Masai people of Africa (top left). He also wears multiple neck rings like the Padaung people of Thailand, as well as a lip plate similar to those of the Kaopo people of Brazil. Le Baaba travels around the United States giving lectures to help others appreciate the cultures of the world as he does. He believes that such lessons in tolerance will go a long way toward securing world peace.

Ties That Bind

During the early 20th century, the Mangbetu people of Central Africa considered elongated skulls a sign of beauty and intelligence. To achieve this highly desirable shape, they bound the heads of infants. In adulthood, both men and women wore hats or grew their hair long and wrapped it around baskets to make their heads look even longer.

CHEEK-KABOB

Participants in the annual nine-day Vegetarian Festival in Phuket, Thailand, skewer themselves instead of the food, puncturing their cheeks with knives, spears, wires, and even broom handles! For weeks before the festival, participants don't smoke, drink alcohol, or eat meat. They think only good thoughts and spend days in deep meditation, often entering trance states. All this is to cleanse their minds in preparation for what lies ahead.

At the beginning of the nine-day festival, male and female participants gather on opposite sides of temple altars to the ringing of bells and beating of drums. Statues of gods, emperors, mythological animals, and other figures are bathed in the flickering light of hundreds of candles. After awhile, participants say they feel spirits taking them over. As soon as that happens, they go outside, where helpers wait to assist in piercing their bodies. Some people are linked together with chains or steel wire. Others are pierced with rods as long as 32 feet, some with heavy objects attached!

After the participants have been pierced, they parade through the streets for hours. They feel that the spirits that inhabit them protect them from pain, and, amazingly, although their skin is repeatedly punctured, there is little bleeding or scarring.

MARKED MEN

As their initiation into adulthood, young men of the Shilluk people of Sudan, Africa, decorate their foreheads with beadlike marks, which are created by filling incisions with gunpowder.

MIRROR, MIRROR!

Fairest of all! Each year the Wodaabe people of West Africa hold beauty contests for men. Bedecked with special makeup, jewelry, charms, and elaborate costumes, the men dance for days to impress the judges, who are two or three beautiful women. Each judge chooses a winner. What does he get as a prize? The judge as his bride!

Waist-ing Away

Ever since she can remember, Cathie Jung of Old Mystic, Connecticut, wished for a tiny waist. In 1983, she decided to go for it and began wearing a corset 23 hours a day, only removing it to take a shower. Twelve years later, she reached her goal—a 15-inch waist that even Scarlett O'Hara could be proud of. Among Jung's many corsets is a sterling silver one that she wears over a black gown for special occasions.

Earning Her Stripes

Ever since she was a little girl, Katzen the Catwoman loved cats—but who knew she would try to become one when she grew up! In fall of 1993, at age 18, Katzen had her arms and legs tattooed with tiger stripes. Nine years later, her tattoos were complete, making her the first woman in history to have a full-body theme tattoo. She even had removable artificial whiskers implanted in her face. Katzen plays bass with her husband in their band, the Human Marvels. By the way, her husband is ThEnigma. He, too, has a full-body theme tattoo—of blue puzzle pieces—as well as implanted Teflon horns!

Designing Woman

When Julia Gnuse was 35, she was diagnosed with porphyria, a condition that affects the skin. The slightest exposure to sunlight caused her skin to blister, leaving her with unsightly scars. To conceal the scars, Gnuse tried tattooing. Nine years and 400 tattoos later, Gnuse's tattoos depict everything from jungle scenes to her favorite actors and cartoon characters. Now she considers her body a living, breathing work of art.

ARTIFICIAL BEAUTY

When a woman in China was disqualified from a beauty contest because she'd had plastic surgery, a new contest was born. Only those who've had cosmetic surgery can apply!

Reaching New Heights

The village of Podoliantsi in the Ukraine is home to someone who just may become the world's tallest man. At age 14, Leonid Stadnik suddenly started growing by leaps and bounds. In 2004, at age 33, he was eight feet four inches tall and still growing. Having already surpassed the height of the current living record holder, the seven-foot-nine-inch-tall Radhouane Charbib of Tunisia, Stadnik is gaining on Robert Wadlow, who at eight feet eleven inches was the tallest man in history. Stadnik, who finds his great height to be a colossal inconvenience, is not interested in setting any records. "Taking a public bus for me is the same as getting into a car's trunk for a normal person," he explains.

Heavy!

In 2004, the Hawaiian-born former Sumo champion Konishiki married Chie Iijima, who weighs a mere 112 pounds. Nicknamed the Dump Truck and Meat Bomb, Konishiki was once the world's heaviest Sumo wrestler, weighing in at more than 600 pounds. Konishiki has been known to down plates of roast chicken, beef, lamb, and fish at one meal. Let's hope that he'll chip in with the cooking!

Hairy!

Formerly a farmer, Tran Van Hay now collects herbs used in traditional medicine and provides them to the people of his region in Vietnam for free. What makes this 67-year-old stand out in a crowd, however, is his extraordinary hair. Tran hasn't been to a barber since 1973, so his hair has had a lot of time to grow. It is now 20 feet long, which exceeds the previous record set in 1997 by Hoo Sateow of Thailand, whose hair was 16 feet 11 inches long.

RIPLEY FILE: 6.24.75

The tail end! Colon T. Updike was known as the "the human horse" because he had a hairy, 18-inch-long tail growing from the middle of his back.

OH, GROW UP!

Jean Bihin of La Reid, Belgium, was so tiny when he was born in 1805, he was not expected to live—yet he grew to a height of eight feet five inches and weighed a whopping 316 pounds.

EXTRA! EXTRA!

Metal Head

When people tell Joe Aylward of Phoenix, Arizona, that he's got holes in his head, they're not kidding. In 1996, Aylward underwent a 90-minute procedure at a piercing salon to embed five metal pieces in his scalp. Now he can screw spikes in a variety of lengths into his shaved head and change his look at will.

About Face

Every two years, men from around the world style their facial hair to compete in one of 17 categories in the World Beard and Moustache Championships.

Hair-raiser

In May 2003, 50-year-old Radhakant Bajpai of Naya Ganj, Uttar Pradesh, India, set a new record for having the longest ear hair. At their longest point, the hairs reached 5.19 inches from the center of Bajpai's outer ear.

Tailor-made

When a child was born in India with a four-inch-long tail at the base of his spine, the news spread rapidly. By 2002, people were coming from far and wide to worship the one-year-old boy, whom many think is the reincarnation of the Hindu god, Hanuman. Named Balaji, which is another name for the monkey-faced god, the child is being exhibited in temples throughout the country. Doctors don't consider Balaji's tail a real tail, because it is made entirely of skin and tissue with no bones. Should Balaji someday decide he would prefer not to have the tail, it could be easily removed.

Face Time

Luis Antonio Aguero Torregosa of Havana, Cuba, has found a way to increase his income: posing with tourists for money. Why is he such an attraction? It must be the more than 300 piercings he has—all on his face!

What a Squirt!

Ilker Yilmaz is able to squirt milk from his eye for an astounding distance of 9.2 feet!

A Living Doll

Since 1989, 49-year-old Cindy Jackson has undergone nine major operations, some of them involving multiple procedures, at a cost of almost $100,000. Why? For beauty's sake: All Jackson's operations were cosmetic! Jackson, who lives in London, England, has had face-lifts, nose jobs, breast implants, and more—and that doesn't count liposuction, chemical peels, and the semi-permanent makeup tattooed on her face. Ouch!

Water on the Brain

Jerome Abramovitch gets a kick out of shocking people. After consulting a doctor, he figured out a way to expand his forehead to five times its normal size. Four hours after injecting a saline solution, his forehead reaches its maximum size. Once all the fluid has been absorbed by his body, it shrinks back to normal. Exactly how Abramovitch achieves his look is a closely-guarded secret.

Splitting Hairs

Composer and pianist Frédéric Chopin (1810–1849) often wore a beard on only one side of his face—the one facing the audience.

Really Big Hair

Born in Australia in 1869, "the Great Unzie" was an albino aborigine who appeared in circus sideshows. His head of hair measured eight feet around!

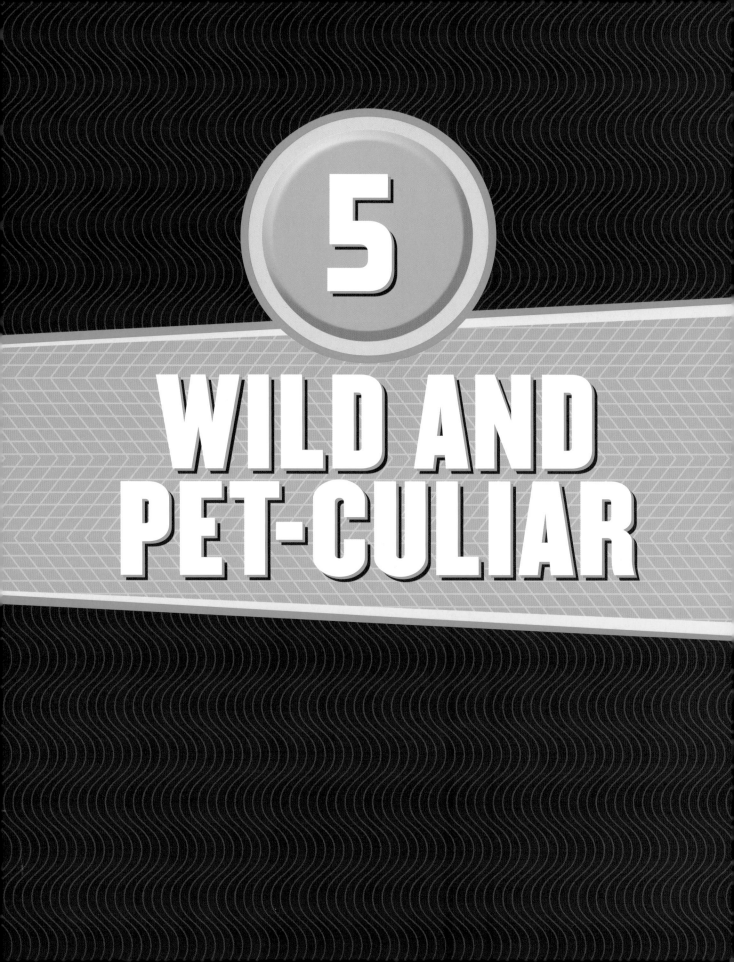

5

WILD AND PET-CULIAR

FREAKY!

Heels Over Head

Born in western Spain, Bufa the lamb has more than four legs to stand on. The placement of her fifth leg may come in handy if she wants to stand on her head!

Double Header

In October 2003, ten-year-old Hunter York of Centertown, Kentucky, found his latest pet in his own backyard. When he picked up the king snake with a stick, he was amazed to find that it had two heads! Luckily, king snakes do not hurt humans, but they do eat poisonous rattlesnakes and copperheads. York named the snake Mary-Kate and Ashley and hopes that it might have a future in show business.

SPARE PARTS

A calf owned by Alex Harpe of Buckely, Michigan, was born with eight legs and two tails.

Beside itself! A pair of tortoises born joined at the belly were successfully separated at an animal hospital in Tempe, Arizona.

Two-faced

You'd have to go pretty far to find another cat like Image, who was born in June 2000 in Bensalem, Pennsylvania. Her owner, Sandra Pyatt, said she didn't notice that Image was different from her littermates until her 12-year-old son, Timothy, called it to her attention. Image was different all right. She had one head but two faces! Since Image has just one brain, both faces blink, yawn, and sneeze at the same time.

MIXED DOUBLES

Cow Licks

For leopards, a cow is usually what's for dinner—not part of its social life. Tell that to a certain leopard in India who's in love with a cow! The feeling seems to be mutual. The cow welcomes her visitor each night in the sugarcane field where she lives, covering it with licks from head to toe. Villagers are happy to have the leopard in their field because as long as it's around, their crops are safe from other animals that might eat or trample them.

MISTAKEN IDENTITY

In Hamburg, Germany, a mixed-up male swan fell head over tail feathers for a swan-shaped pedal boat, chasing away anyone who tried to get near it!

Baby Le Pew

No, you're not seeing things. This cat is nursing an orphaned baby skunk that was brought to her by animal control officers in Corpus Christi, Texas. Though the cat has no home of her own and lives at the pound, she was purr-fectly content to make room for another baby.

RIPLEY FILE: 2.21.04

How moo-ving! An Angus cow in New Zealand took pity on an orphaned lamb and adopted her, allowing the lamb to nurse along with her own calf.

Such Deer Friends

Several German children were playing in the woods when they spied a two-week-old fawn nestled in some leaves. Since the orphan would have starved on her own, the children scooped her up and gave her to their animal-loving neighbor, Wilfried Siebert. Siebert's hunting dog, Jesse, had just given birth to three pups and seemed delighted to adopt a fourth. The fact that the adopted baby was a fawn made no difference to Jesse, who nursed the fawn right along with her own pups!

DOGGONE SMART!

Ramping It Up

A baby elephant in Amboseli National Park in Kenya, Africa, recently had a close call when he fell into a mud hole and couldn't get out. His mother was unable to get him out by herself, so she called for help with a series of loud trumpets. In no time, two adult elephants heeded her call. Together, the three adults began digging with feet and tusks until they had constructed a ramp. Then out walked the baby on his own private elephant walk!

RIPLEY FILE: 11.6.67

Well balanced!
Tim, a horse owned by J. D. Wilton of Australia, could balance his entire weight on one small wooden block while his rider stood up in the saddle, twirling a lasso!

Crow's Feat

British researchers were surprised to find out that crows not only know how to use tools but also how to make them! First, they presented a caged crow with a puzzle—how to get corn kernels out of a clear plastic tube. They provided her with straight and curved wires. The crow chose the curved wire and retrieved her reward. Next, she was presented with the same problem, but this time given a straight wire only. The crow, undaunted, used her beak to bend the wire so that the tool would work for her. Not bad for a birdbrain!

Fetch!

Meet Rico, a border collie who lives near the Max Planck Institute for Evolutionary Anthropology in Leipzig, Germany. Rico knows the names of some 200 toys and will retrieve whichever one you ask for. Not only that, but in a test where an unfamiliar object was mixed in with nine known objects, Rico was able to associate the new word with the unfamiliar object. Four months later, with no further exposure to it, Rico was able to remember the name of the new object and single it out from others. Scientists say that Rico's comprehension is roughly equivalent to that of the average three-year-old. Not all dogs have Rico's smarts, but this one certainly proves he is no "dumb animal!"

BIRDBRAIN

Puck, a parrot owned by Camille Jordan of Petaluma, California, had a vocabulary of 1,728 words when it died in 1994!

THAT'S FISHY!

Tongue Depressors

The tongue-biting isopod is a crustacean (hard-shelled sea creature) with a lot of crust! First it invades a fish's mouth and causes its tongue to fall out. Then it camps out where the tongue used to be. The fish uses the isopod's hard back to crush its dinner, while the isopod feeds on the fish's blood and the mucous in its mouth.

CHAMP-ANZEE

Nim, a chimpanzee tutored by Susan Quimby at Columbia University, mastered sign language and could communicate using a 95-word vocabulary.

Body Snatchers

Before her eggs hatch, a female crab carries them in a brood pouch attached to her belly. Sometimes, a female larva of a parasitic barnacle burrows inside a crab, settles in its belly, and forms a knob where the crab's brood pouch would be. Once a male parasitic barnacle enters a tiny hole in the knob, he makes himself at home inside the female barnacle and fertilizes her eggs. The crab treats the larvae-filled knob just like it would a brood pouch, protecting it from predators and stroking it to keep it clean. When the barnacle larvae are fully developed, the crab expels them with contractions, effectively giving birth to creatures that are not its own!

Gutsy Move

A starfish has the bizarre ability to turn its stomach inside out, thrust it out through its mouth, and digest its prey outside its body.

Major sibling rivalry! Embryonic sand tiger sharks battle each other inside the womb until only one shark is left!

Blowhards

Although herrings don't have vocal cords, they have a very effective way of communicating. They pass gas! A Canadian research team led by marine biologist Ben Wilson, caught herrings and put them in large tanks to study them. What they saw was some pretty strange behavior. At night the fish would gulp air at the surface, store it, then release it through their rear ends. The noise they made helped the fish find each other in the dark without alerting predators.

SILLY PET TRICKS

Tall Tails

German animal trainers Maike and Jorg Probst have created a circus act that is a towering success. They've trained Gockel the rooster to fly onto the shoulders of Klausi the monkey, who sits on the back of Paul the goat, who stands on the back of Piccolo the donkey.

SPEAK!

Gypsy, a dog owned by Preston Cathcart, asks for food by distinctly saying, "I want some."

On a Roll

Birling is a sport in which a competitor tries to balance on a floating log while spinning it with his or her feet. Peppy, a Dalmatian belonging to professional "birler" Bill Fontana of Fort Frances, Ontario, Canada, gave his owner a run for his money by rolling a log for one mile in an hour's time!

Jumping for Joy

Brutus is a miniature dachshund with no fear of heights. His owner, skydiver Ron Sirull, couldn't get Brutus to stop chasing his plane down the runway any time he left to go skydiving. So Sirull finally gave in and on May 1, 1997, he tucked the little dog into a pouch on his chest and took him skydiving. Now Brutus is a pro, with more than 100 jumps under his collar.

RIPLEY FILE:
4.6.04

Walking the line! Elephants were trained by the ancient Romans to perform on the tightrope.

From Trees to Skis

After they adopted a baby squirrel that had fallen out of its nest, Chuck and Lou Ann Best found they had their hands full. Their new pet, named Twiggy, was getting into everything! Maybe she's bored, they thought. The Bests loved to water-ski, so they made Twiggy a pair of tiny skis and fastened her to a remote-controlled toy motorboat. Each time Twiggy completed a lap around the pool, she got a treat. Since then, the Bests have adopted other abandoned baby squirrels and taught them to water-ski. Now the Best squirrels are on the road, performing at boat shows and on TV.

EXTRA! EXTRA!

Little Squawks on the Prairie

Northern Arizona University professor Con Slobodchikoff is an expert on prairie dogs. What he's found is truly astonishing: Prairie dogs have their own language. Slobodchikoff has distinguished ten different calls used to identify specific intruders, including humans, hawks, elk, and coyotes, as well as distinct calls describing such characteristics as color, size, and shape!

What an Earful!

In the spring of 2004, there was a flood of calls to an animal shelter in Germany. Why? Everyone was anxious to adopt Lilly, a kitten whose picture was in all the papers. The one-of-a-kind kitty had been born with four ears, two on either side of her head—though she can only hear through the front pair.

Bear Handed

England's King Henry III kept a pet bear that regularly went fishing in the Thames River.

Rat Race

In 2003, auditions were held throughout Europe for the part of Scabbers in the film *Harry Potter and the Prisoner of Azkaban*. Based on their resemblance to each other and their winning personalities, two rats from the Berlin Zoo got the part. When the filming was over, the rats did not go back to the zoo. Why? Actor Rupert Grint, who plays Ron Weasley in the movie, became so attached to his furry little co-stars that he decided to take them home.

Hot-rod-ent!

Tourists at a seaside resort in Cleveleys, England, were astonished to see a hamster whiz by in a toy racecar. The mini hot rod had been fitted with a hamster exercise wheel, so when the hamster pumped its little legs, the car zipped right along. Someone managed to catch the little speedster and turned it in to the police, who nicknamed it Speedy and turned it over to the local RSPCA (Royal Society for the Prevention of Cruelty to Animals).

Cat-a-comb

Cats were so revered in ancient Siam that when a member of royalty died, his or her Siamese cat was buried in the same tomb. Luckily for the cat, the tomb was equipped with tunnels that allowed the cat to escape and be carried to a temple where it was protected for life.

Fast Kibbles

Maggie Patterson's drive-through restaurant in Niles, Michigan, serves all-natural fast food for dogs! It's even shaped like pizza, fries, and other people-food!

Top Dog

Benji, a collie owned by Olive Pedley of Great Britain, can fetch objects even in the dark and can recognize over 50 different names.

The Cat's Meow

In 2002, Nicholas Nicastro, a graduate student in psychology at Cornell University, conducted a test to find out whether cats choose their meows to be pleasing to humans. He recorded 100 different calls from 12 different cats and asked volunteers to rate them for pleasantness. He says that the meows considered most appealing were the shorter ones that went from a high to a low pitch—exactly the kind of inviting meows you hear in animal shelters from cats hoping to be adopted!

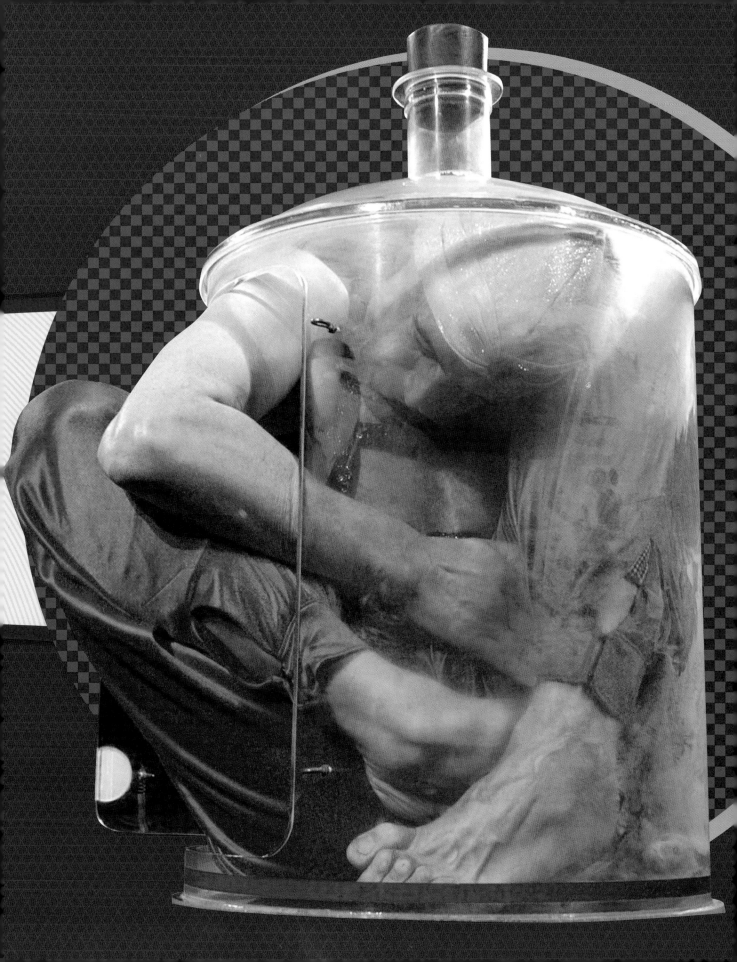

WILD ESCAPES!

Hole-y Matrimony

In late 2003, a male tourist must have missed the signs posted in Australia's Burleigh Heads National Park warning visitors to beware of wild brush-turkeys. Too bad! If he'd noticed them, perhaps he would have been more careful. To attract a mate, a male brush-turkey digs a hole in the ground, then fills it with vegetation to form a large mound, which will eventually be used to incubate the mate's eggs. Apparently, one male brush-turkey had just finished digging its 9-foot-deep hole when the man came along and fell in. Undeterred, the bird piled vegetation into the hole until it covered the man up to his head. He remained there until he was discovered and rescued by an emergency team!

Not-So-Happy Camper

One spring day in 2004, a 15-year-old boy woke up in his tent at a wilderness camp in Anchorage, Alaska, to find a big brown bear sitting next to him. The boy ran out of the tent, but the bear gave chase, biting him several times on the back. Finally, the boy managed to get an air horn from his backpack and blew it directly into the bear's face. The noise awakened everyone in the camp. Not until counselors blasted the bear with pepper spray and hurled flares at its feet did it finally give up and run away. After the young camper was airlifted to a hospital, he made a full recovery.

HANGIN' TOUGH

On October 31, 2003, 13-year-old Bethany Hamilton, one of the best amateur female surfers in Hawaii, was resting on her surfboard, waiting for a wave. Suddenly, a huge tiger shark latched on to Bethany's left arm just inches below the shoulder and began yanking her around. She clung to the board, and the shark finally let go—but not until it had torn off most of her arm.

When Bethany called for help, a friend's father, who was surfing nearby, wrapped his T-shirt around the wound and helped her get to shore. There he fashioned a tourniquet from his surfboard leash to stop the bleeding. Without the tourniquet, doctors say that Bethany would have bled to death.

During Bethany's hospital stay, everyone was amazed by her upbeat attitude. The only time she got upset was when she learned that fishermen were planning to hunt down the 13-foot-long, 1,500-pound tiger shark that had attacked her. Bethany refused to rest until she was assured that the animal would not be harmed.

Determined to do everything she did before the attack, Bethany was back in the water surfing less than a month later and competing again by January. Now an honorary member of the United States Triathlon Team, Bethany looks forward to future competitions. Most would agree that whether she wins or not, Bethany Hamilton will always be a champion.

SEALED WITH A KISS

Downy Ferrer of Laguna Hills, California, had to be rescued by paramedics after she kissed her pet turtle. Why? Because it clamped on to her upper lip and wouldn't let go!

LITTLEST SURVIVORS

Hot Lunch

Teardrop, the boa constrictor, is such a valued member of the Probst family of Klamath Falls, Oregon, that she rarely spends time in her tank. One day, the Probsts spotted something strange hanging out of her mouth. It was a power cord! Teardrop had apparently mistaken an electric heating pad for lunch. Ron Probst rushed the listless boa to the Basin Animal Hospital. Thankfully, after two hours of surgery and several months' recovery time, Teardrop was back to her old slinky self.

MADE A BIG SQUAWK!

When a fire blazed through Ye Olde Cheshire Cheese Pub in Derbyshire, England, Henry, the owner's parrot, squawked "Hello" until a firefighter rescued him.

Hoodwinked

On a cold and snowy February day in 2004, a cat in Vienna, Austria, found the perfect place to keep warm—inside someone's car engine. Unaware that he had a passenger, the driver got in and drove off. He picked up speed on the highway but realized too late how slippery the road was when he skidded and crashed into another car. When he opened the hood to investigate a hissing noise, he saw the cat. Only after part of the engine was removed at a service station could they get the cat out. The little stowaway had survived a 40-mile drive and a high-speed crash, all while riding under the hood of a car!

Sling Shot

Regular customers at the Sky Port Diner in Scotia, New York, were used to watching Dick, the owner's 17-year-old goldfish, swim happily in his tank on the counter. So in November 2003, when the eight-inch-long fish got swim bladder disease and could barely stay afloat, they pitched in to give him a shot at recovery. Three times a day, they took turns hand-feeding Dick a diet of cooked peas prescribed by a veterinary student. Then they used gauze, drinking straws, string, and fishing bobbers to create a sling so the fish could continue to swim while he recovered. The treatment worked, and Dick is back to swimming all on his own.

RIPLEY FILE: 1.23.04

Doggone! When a huge hole suddenly opened up in Sharon and Mark Whitelaw's garden in Moxley, England, their dog Toby tumbled in. He fell 20 feet into a ventilation shaft of an old mine! Amazingly, Toby survived.

WACKY!

Nailed!

On April 19, 2004, Isidro Mejia was working at a construction site in the Antelope Valley, north of Los Angeles, California, when he tripped and fell off the roof of the house onto a coworker who was using a nail gun. As the two tumbled to the ground, the nail gun went off, driving six 3.5-inch nails into Mejia's head and neck. Three of the nails entered his brain and one entered his spine at the base of the skull. Miraculously, the nails missed his brain stem and spinal cord, where they would certainly have caused paralysis or death. Still, it was tricky for doctors at the Providence Holy Cross Medical Center to remove the nails successfully. Within a couple of weeks, however, Mejia was able to walk and speak slowly, and is expected to make a full recovery.

Human Genie

Circus performer Hugo Zamoratte of Argentina has a strange workplace— the inside of a bottle. To accommodate the tight fit, this former gymnast dislocates every bone in his body except for his fingers, toes, and backbone. One time, while practicing his act in a hotel room, Zamoratte became trapped when the door in the side of the bottle snapped shut. Luckily for Zamoratte, a timely visit from a hotel maid kept him from suffocating!

Child's Play

For about an hour in January 2004, an arcade machine at a Piggly Wiggly grocery store in Sheboygan, Wisconsin, contained more than stuffed animals. Seven-year-old Timmy Novotny was also inside. While his father talked on a nearby phone, Timmy decided to do some exploring. Like a little Houdini, the child managed to squeeze himself through the 8-by-10-inch opening that dispensed the toys. By the time his father saw him, Timmy was stuck inside the glass enclosure. It took the expertise of a locksmith to free Timmy, who explained, "I just wanted to go in there 'cause I thought I could slip back out, but I couldn't."

RIPLEY FILE: 7.11.65

Master of disaster! Frank Tower, who worked as an oiler on ships, swam away from three major shipwrecks and lived to tell the tale: the *Titanic* in 1912, the *Empress of Ireland* in 1914, and the *Lusitania* in 1915!

HOUSEBROKEN

Egon Selestrin of Croatia was watching TV in his living room when a 200-foot-long ship crashed through the wall of his beachfront home. Luckily, Selestrin managed to get out of his house before the whole structure collapsed.

EXTRA! EXTRA!

Whoosh!

In 1991, John David Bridges, a flight engineer for 20 years, was inspecting a plane on the deck of the U.S.S. *Roosevelt* aircraft carrier when the unthinkable happened. He was sucked into the air intake of a jet engine. Flames shot out of the back of the plane as the engine spit out the clothes he was wearing! Unbelievable as it seems, Bridges survived the accident with only a fractured collarbone and punctured eardrum to show for it. He was saved because he was wedged against the turbine's nose cone—the only place where he could have survived!

Between Iraq and a Hard Place

Troops in Southampton, England, had a surprise waiting for them when they looked inside a British army tank that had just arrived home from Iraq. There, squealing plaintively, was a starving kitten, so small she had to be fed milk with a syringe. She was nicknamed "The Kitten of Mass Destruction" because as soon as she started feeling better, she got her paws into everything.

Out on a Limb

Catalin Pavel of Mangalia, Romania, discovered he was afraid of heights only after he had climbed 70 feet up a tree in order to rescue a cat. Pavel spent all day and all night in the tree until a neighbor heard him yelling for help and called firefighters to get him and his feline friend down.

Fish Breath

Leo van Aert of Belgium used to drive an ambulance for a living, so he knew just what to do when his pet fish, a koi carp, began thrashing around in the pond, then stopped moving altogether. Van Aert lifted the carp from the water and gave it a heart massage. When that didn't work, he gave it mouth-to-mouth resuscitation. The fish revived and has been doing swimmingly ever since.

Gnawing Problem

After Australian Luke Tresoglavic was treated with antibiotics, he made a full recovery from a painful shark bite. That was the easy part. Getting the shark to let go in the first place was a whole lot harder! The victim had been swimming in waters north of Sydney, when a small shark sank its teeth into his leg and would not let go—not even as Tresoglavic swam to shore or as he walked to his car. It even hung on while he drove himself to the clubhouse. Luckily, lifeguards there knew just what to do. They hosed it down with water until the stubborn fish finally gave up and let go!

Had a Great Fall

In 1997, Carol Murray of Bradford, Ontario, Canada, was skydiving for the first time when her parachute failed to open. After plunging 3,200 feet, she landed on a wet lawn, just missing a tree, a house, and a driveway. Though seriously injured, Murray survived and, after years of physical therapy, is now able to walk again.

Water Hazard

Roy Williams of Georgia survived after being bitten in the head by a rattlesnake while retrieving his golf ball from some wetlands.

7

DEAD ZONE

ANIMAL PRESERVES

Getting Stuffed

Tia Resleure shares her San Francisco home with close to 100 animals. Most of them are dead. That's because Resleure is an artist who has figured out how to use taxidermy in her artwork. Her obsession with taxidermy began when she first laid eyes on her grandfather's collection. Now she does custom work for people all over the world. After each animal has been stuffed, Resleure dresses it in clothing befitting its personality and arranges it in its own personalized diorama.

STAY!

A California company called Genetic Savings and Clone provides a unique service for bereaved pet owners—for a mere $50,000 per animal, they will clone your pet!

Long Shelf Life

In 1936, the Tasmanian tiger became officially extinct. Every last one had been hunted down by farmers who blamed the wolf-sized marsupial for killing their sheep. Recently, Mike Archer, director of the Australian Museum in Sydney, took steps to clone the animal. In May 2000, a research team extracted DNA from a Tasmanian tiger pup that had been preserved in formaldehyde for the museum's collection. Two years later, the animal's genes were successfully replicated. Soon the call of the Tasmanian tiger may be heard again.

Oh, Dry Up!

Richard Gurnee of Watsonville, California, has a new idea about what to do with roadkill. He freeze-dries the bodies of squirrels, raccoons, skunks, bobcats, and other unfortunate creatures who have met their end on the pavement, as well as animals provided by hunters. When done correctly, freeze-drying can give more natural-looking results than taxidermy. Gurnee's two-step process involves placing the body in a freezer set at 50 degrees below zero, then dehydrating it in a drying cylinder. He knows all bodily fluids are gone when the corpse stops losing weight. Gurnee crafts molds for the eyes from coffee lids, then casts them in polyester and resin. Irises are made from colored cardboard. The finished animals often end up in display cases in schools, museums, and nature centers.

RIPLEY FILE:
12.27.98

Game over! In Cornwall, England, there is a pet cemetery with a section devoted entirely to electronic Tamagotchi pets.

SPOOKED!

Up in Smoke

In the seventh month of each lunar year, according to an ancient Chinese custom, the dead rise out of the underworld to make an appearance on Earth. Many Chinese are afraid to venture out at this time, and attribute anything bad that happens to these restless souls. To keep the spirits friendly, Chinese celebrate Yu Lan Pen, or the Festival of the Hungry Ghosts, entertaining the spirits with concerts and presenting them with intricate paper replicas of favorite possessions, such as laptops, cell phones, TVs, and stereo equipment. When the moon is full, they burn the paper offerings in huge bonfires that can be seen for miles around.

STIFF COMPETITION

Cassadaga is a town in Florida where nearly all the residents are mediums or psychics—people whose main business is communicating with the dead!

Favorite Haunt

England's Hampton Court was home to Henry VIII, a king known for beheading anyone who crossed him, so it's not surprising that people believe disgruntled souls roam the halls. In December 2003, guards were alerted by alarms that a set of fire doors had been opened, but when they went to check, the doors were closed. Puzzled, they examined closed-circuit TV footage and were astounded to see the locked doors fly open all by themselves. Moments later, they were even more astounded to see a ghostly figure dressed in a robelike garment suddenly appear and close the doors! Was it a real ghost or a prank? You be the judge.

Ship of Ghouls

From her maiden voyage in 1936 to her final one in 1967, about 50 people perished aboard the *Queen Mary*. Today, the ship serves as a floating hotel in Long Beach, California, and guests staying there have reported seeing the ghosts of these casualties in such areas as the indoor first-class pool, the royal theater, and the boiler room, as well as on the decks. The hotel even offers a Ghost Encounters Tour of the ship!

Flying High

"Steady" Ed Headrick, the inventor who helped perfect the Frisbee and the father of disc golf (a kind of Frisbee game), died in 2002 at age 78. True to his wishes, his family had his ashes incorporated into special memorial discs. Headrick's wife, Farina, and her son tossed the first disc back and forth, fulfilling another of his wishes: that he could fly. Limited edition discs are sold in sets of two—one to play with and one to keep—for $210 by the Disc Golf Association. Proceeds go into a nonprofit "Steady" Ed Memorial Fund or toward a "Steady" Ed Memorial Museum.

The Lines of Headrick Memorial Freestyle Disc

June 28, 1924
to
August 12, 2002

Herein lie the ashes of "Steady" Ed, founding father of Frisbee and the sport of Disc Golf.

A Giant of a man who was many things to many people.

Fly Free and rest in peace.

GRAVE THOUGHTS

Robert Barrows of California has filed for a patent on a new kind of tombstone, equipped with a video that displays a pre-recorded message from the person who is buried in the grave.

Lasting Impression

Now thanks to the Meadow Hill Company in Fox River Grove, Illinois, grieving relatives can take home a one-of-a-kind keepsake to remember a loved one—a pendant imprinted with his or her thumbprint. Called Thumbies, the pendants are created when a wax casting of the deceased loved-one's thumbprint is made into a gold or silver piece of jewelry.

Frozen Stiff

When his grandfather died at the age of 89, Trygve Bauge, formerly of Nederland, Colorado, had him cryogenically preserved in nitrogen and stuck him in a shed. Since moving to Norway, Bauge pays someone to regularly haul dry ice to the makeshift tomb to keep Grandpa cold until the day science comes up with a way to bring him back to life. Meanwhile, citizens of Nederland have seen fit to celebrate this quirky fact with a festival called Frozen Dead Guy Days. There's something for everyone—coffin races, a Grandpa look-alike competition, frozen-drink guzzling contests, and, of course, a parade.

REMAINS OF THE DAY

5000 B.C.E.

The Chinchorros, who lived more than 7,000 years ago in what is now northern Chile, took apart their corpses, chemically treated the internal organs, and put all the pieces back together again. Then they covered the bodies with clay and decorated them with painted or carved designs.

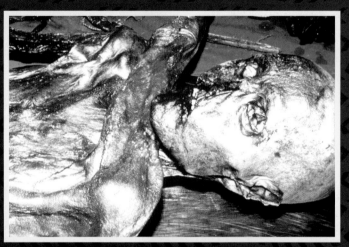

3300 B.C.E.

About 5,300 years ago, high in the mountains of the Ötzal Alps, a 45-year-old man was struck in the shoulder by an arrow. His frozen body lay facedown where he died until September 19, 1991, when Helmut and Erika Simon, who were hiking on the border of Austria and Italy, stumbled across him. The mummy (above), nicknamed Ötzi, turned out to be the oldest, best-preserved ice mummy found to date.

496 B.C.E.

In northern Chile about 2,500 years ago, a boy died and was buried. Fast forward to the town of Arica in 2003. Two dogs owned by Ivan Paredes are digging for a bone in their backyard. Suddenly they start to bark. Imagine Paredes's surprise when he goes to investigate and discovers what the dogs have dug up! The boy's mummy, which was in surprisingly good condition, is now in the San Miguel de Azapa Museum.

ca. C.E. 50

Like ice mummies, bog mummies are created by nature. That's because conditions in a bog—cold water containing tannic acid from plants—are just right for preserving bodies. In 1897, a nearly 2,000-year-old mummy (far left) of a 16-year-old girl who had been stabbed and strangled was discovered in a bog in the Netherlands. In 1992, a medical artist named Richard Neave was able to reconstruct the girl's face (left) using wax, clay, additional hair, and a pair of artificial eyes.

1000 B.C.E.

The Taklimakan Desert is a vast dry area of shifting sand dunes in western China—perfect for preserving the bodies of the dead. Since the 1970s, archaeologists have unearthed a number of well-preserved mummies, many still dressed in their hats, boots, and colorful robes—like the mummy of a 58-year-old woman (right) found in the village of Zaghunluq in 1985.

100–1300

The Anasazi people, who lived in the American Southwest for about 1,200 years, wrapped their dead in fur and laid them to rest in caves or shallow recesses in cliffs. Often, the mummies were given brand-new sandals, probably to take their first steps in the next world.

1500

A little more than 500 years ago, the Incas were still making human sacrifices. In 1999, Johan Reinhard came upon three mummies of children on a mountaintop shrine in Peru. Each had perfect features—further supporting researchers' belief that the Incas chose their most beautiful children for religious sacrifice!

EXTRA! EXTRA!

Tick Tock

Hannah Beswick of Sale, England, left a fortune to her physician—with the condition that he look upon her face once each year as long as he lived! Her embalmed body was kept in the case of a grandfather clock for 101 years!

Dead Beats

Jazz funerals are a unique New Orleans tradition. When old-time jazz musicians die, a brass band often accompanies the funeral procession to the cemetery. On the way in, they play slow, heart-rending dirges. Once the body has been laid to rest, however, they swing into such lively numbers as "When the Saints Go Marching In" to celebrate the release of the deceased's soul.

Curses!

Ever since the day 138 years ago when the Reverend Thomas Baker was killed by cannibals in the tiny Fijian village of Nabutautau, residents have had nothing but bad luck. In addition to suffering extremes in weather, they have been regularly overlooked by a government that has not yet built them good roads or hooked them up with electricity. In 2003, Baker's descendants were invited to Nabutautau to receive an official apology in the hope that Baker's avenging spirit would lift the curse on the town.

Ice Maiden

In the mountains of southern Siberia, local officials have started a petition to make sure that the 2,500-year-old ice mummy of a tattooed princess unearthed by archaeologists in 1993 is reburied as soon as possible. They are hoping that this will put an end to the constant earthquakes that have been plaguing their region.

Lighting the Way

A company in Austria makes solar-powered, glow-in-the-dark gravestones that light up at night.

Highway to Heaven

In 2003, a 2,500-year-old chariot was unearthed by workers who were building a highway through northern England. Amazingly, the chariot's wheels were still intact! Even more amazing were the chariot's contents—the remains of a man in his 30s! Experts believe he was a tribal chief, since not everyone would have been afforded the honor of being buried in a chariot.

Winging It

It's common knowledge that the ancient Egyptians admired cats and were often buried with them. However, not many people know that Egyptians also held falcons in very high esteem and that they were mummified and buried with royalty as well. The ancient Egyptians believed that the eyes of falcons held the power of the sun and the moon, making them the perfect guides for pharaohs in the afterlife.

Toasting a Ghost

On the occasion of her death in 2004 in Junin, Peru, Olga Riva's friends were determined to honor a pact they'd made with her. So they whisked her from the morgue, propped her up at their favorite haunt, and toasted her with drinks!

Keeping an Eye Out

The last grand lama of Mongolia was mummified with his eyes open and a lifelike smile. Covered from head to toe with gold, he sits outside the Choijin Monastery-Museum in Ulan Bator.

Dead Man Breathing

In January 2004, a hospital sent a dead man to the Muffley Funeral Home in New Mexico. Imagine the surprise of owner Russell Muffley when the dead man began breathing on the preparation table. Muffley immediately started CPR and continued until the ambulance arrived to take the "dead" man back to the hospital.

8

LOONY LUCK

OH, NO!

Unlucky Break

In December 2003, an official at the Thai Culture Ministry received a shard of decorative glass in the mail. It seems that two years earlier, the polygon-shaped fragment had broken off Bangkok's Temple of the Emerald Buddha, Thailand's most sacred shrine. A German tourist found it, picked it up, and put it in his pocket. Afterward, the tourist, who had always considered himself a lucky man, had nothing but bad luck. Hoping to break the spell, he returned the glass with a note asking the official to put it back where it belongs.

FOUR-BIDDEN

Public buildings in China rarely have an official fourth floor because the Chinese character for the number four is the same as the character for death.

Coat of Doom

Jabez Spicer of Leyden, Massachusetts, was killed by two bullets on January 25, 1787, in Shays' Rebellion at Springfield Arsenal. Jabez was wearing the coat his brother Daniel had been wearing when he was killed by two bullets on March 5, 1784. The bullets that killed Jabez passed through the same two holes that had been made when Daniel was killed three years earlier!

RIPLEY FILE: 9.18.38

Fateful Friday! The only seven-masted schooner that ever sailed the seas was named after Thomas W. Lawson, author of *Friday the Thirteenth*. Oddly enough, the ship was wrecked in a storm on Friday, December 13, 1907.

Curse of the Quarters

Shortly after their commemorative quarters were issued, several states had a run of bad luck. Right after New Hampshire's distinctive rock formation, known as the Old Man of the Mountain, was featured on the quarter, it crumbled to dust. Soon after Maryland's statehouse appeared on that state's quarter, it was struck by lightning. In Georgia, peach production suffered after a peach was featured on the state quarter, and the Vermont maple syrup industry suffered losses after being celebrated on the Vermont quarter. In fact, bad luck related to the images on their quarters has affected three out of every four states!

OOPS!

Fangs a Lot!

A thief got the surprise of his life when he swiped a canvas bag from the passenger seat of a car stopped at a traffic light In Sydney, Australia. It turned out the driver was a professional snake catcher who had just captured a venomous red-bellied black snake. Police warned city residents to be on the lookout for a loose reptile. *Hiss!*

REAL CLIFFHANGER

A map of a mountain trail printed in a British hiking magazine recommended a route that would actually lead climbers straight off the edge of a cliff! Thankfully, it was corrected before anyone got hurt.

A Taste of Money

Hoping to safeguard his earnings, a bicycle repairman in China hid the equivalent of $900 in yuan under his mattress. Months later, when he decided to deposit the cash in his savings account, he found that much of it had been chewed up. The suspects: Termites. The evidence: Termite wings on the cash. The verdict: Guilty!

RIPLEY FILE: 1.9.04

Trashed! Ezekiel Garnett and his sister Karen of Chicago, Illinois, accidentally threw out a winning lottery ticket worth 10.5 million dollars. Luckily, they managed to retrieve it before sanitation workers carted it away.

Great Ball of Fire

Firefighter Jimmy Gibson of Shawnee, Oklahoma, determined that a fire in a couch was started by a crystal ball that acted like a magnifying glass when left in direct sunlight.

Up a Creek

One day in February 2003, two dogs were having the time of their lives chasing a deer across a field, through the woods, and into Peachblossom Creek—and that's when the dogs' luck ran out. They got stuck on the cracking ice, unable to take even one more step. Their owner, Eric Hartge, went after them in his kayak, and— Believe It or Not!—he got stranded, too. The trio was rescued, but it took the Easton Volunteer Fire Department three helicopters and a boat to do the job!

PERFECT TIMING

RIPLEY FILE:
7.20.75

Jail quake! Gabriel Magalhaens (1609–1677), a Portuguese missionary to China, was arrested six times by Chinese authorities for preaching his religion and received a death sentence all six times. On the night before each execution, however, an earthquake demolished his prison and set him free.

Baby Boon

The D'Onofrios of Brewster, New York, try to stay one step ahead of their active toddler, Billy, who likes to push buttons on appliances. The phones are put out of his reach to keep him from making random calls, and tape covers the controls on the sound system and TV. Luckily, they forgot to hide the remote, because when Billy took it apart in January 2004, out fell a battery—a purple battery labeled "winner." Billy's mom took the battery to the Toys "R" Us where she'd bought it, thinking she might get a coupon or a package of free batteries. Imagine her surprise when she found out that the special AAA Duracell battery was part of a promotional campaign—and worth $100,000!

Really Happy Meal

When Florida resident Janice Meissner ordered breakfast at a McDonald's drive-through window in December 2003, she got quite a surprise. Instead of her meal, the bag she was given was filled with thousands of dollars. After Meissner returned the cash in exchange for her food, she received a thank you note and a $50 McDonald's gift certificate. The reward may have been small potatoes, but it sure bought lots of fries!

Really Intensive Care

Dorothy Fletcher of Liverpool, England, was on her way to her daughter's wedding when she had a heart attack on the airplane. A flight attendant asked whether there was a doctor available, and with that, no fewer than 15 heart specialists rushed to Fletcher's rescue! It turned out the doctors were flying to a cardiology convention in Orlando, Florida. Had Fletcher had the attack on any other plane, she might not have survived. After three days in the hospital, she was well enough to attend the wedding.

HEAVEN SENT

In 1991, Sergeant Rory Lomas of Savannah, Georgia, who was stationed in Saudi Arabia, received a letter addressed "To Any Soldier." Believe It or Not!, the letter was signed by his own 10-year-old daughter, who was fulfilling a class assignment!

HOW ABOUT THAT!

Catching Up

The last time Gilbert Fogg saw his friend Tom Parker, they were both in Anzio, Italy, fighting shoulder to shoulder in one of the bloodiest battles of World War II. That was in 1944. Both were injured, and each thought the other had died. In 2004, Fogg moved into a new retirement apartment in Nettleham, England. Who was his next-door neighbor? None other than his long-lost buddy, Tom Parker! Once they started talking, they couldn't stop. After all, they had 60 years of stories to tell.

All Bottled Up

What are the chances of a bottle tossed into the sea ending up in the hands of the thrower's son 20 years later? Highly unlikely? Think again! In 2003, Dr. Brian Ardel of Port Charlotte, Florida, was strolling on an island in the Bahamas when he found a green bottle in the sand. Inside was a note dated September 8, 1983, giving the name James Striffler and an address. After arriving home, Ardel located James Striffler on the Internet. Jim's late father, John Striffler, had written a message to his son and tossed the bottle into the ocean while on a cruise. Just that day, before receiving Ardel's call, Jim had lit a candle for his father for All Soul's Day. In Jim's own words, getting the note was like "getting a little piece of my father back."

LOST AND FOUND

At her 20th birthday party in 2002, Hofstra University junior Tamara Rabi received a gift that outshone all the others. One of the guests said she looked just like a friend of his. As they talked, Tamara learned not only that her look-alike, Adriana Scott, had been born and adopted in Guadalajara, Mexico—just as she had—but also had the same birthday. Soon the young women had each other's e-mail addresses.

Before Adriana could e-mail Tamara, her mother told her what she'd held back for 20 years—that Adriana had a twin she'd wanted to adopt but couldn't. Tamara and Adriana agreed to meet. As they walked toward each other for the first time, the sisters were astonished to see that each possessed the same heart-shaped face and almond-shaped brown eyes. They were identical in every way—even down to the patterns on the palms of their hands.

It turned out both women had been raised in New York only 20 miles apart, Tamara in Manhattan and Adriana in Valley Stream. At the time of their meeting, both women were attending colleges on Long Island.

Tamara and Adriana were raised as only children, so they are learning for the first time what it's like to be and to have a twin sister sharing many of the same idiosyncrasies, as well as likes and dislikes. Starting from scratch is never easy, but they are finding the rewards are well worth the effort. Both are keenly aware that, were it not for the chance meeting with a mutual acquaintance, they might never have met.

HAPPY, HAPPY, HAPPY BIRTHDAY!

Angela Close of Victoria, Australia, gave birth to a baby girl on Christmas Day, the same day she and her own mother, Jean Carr, were born. The odds of that happening are 48 million to one!

EXTRA! EXTRA!

Taking a Dive

Every night before a game, Mark Van Eeghen, formerly a running back for the Oakland Raiders football team, would dive from his television set to his bed for good luck.

Surprising Development!

When Cliff Harris of Sanford-on-Thames, England, bought a box of camera equipment at a thrift shop and developed the roll of old film inside, he discovered a photograph of himself as a boy, taken 50 years earlier!

Double Dealing

What are the odds? A driver passing through Chapleau, Ontario, Canada, was given a ticket by a police officer who looked exactly like the officer who'd given him a ticket three weeks earlier in British Columbia, Canada, about 3,000 miles away. It turned out the officers were twin brothers—and the man behind the wheel was a speedy driver!

Go Directly to Jail!

Samuel Jones of White Hall, Arkansas, was able to identify the thief who stole his car when the thief pulled up in the stolen vehicle and asked Jones for directions!

I HAD A CAR JUST LIKE THIS!

Un-kin-ny!

Acquaintances of Pauline E. Taylor and Pauline Taylor of Detroit, Michigan, are amazed to discover that these women are not related in any way. The reason for their astonishment? In addition to sharing exactly the same birth date, the women look enough alike to be twins. They even have the same taste in dress, food, clothing, and hobbies. Unbelievable? Believe It!

Nonchal-ant

In 1989, Kathryn Fuller, president of the World Wildlife Federation, discovered a new species of ant. Where did she find it? It was crawling across her desk!

Look for the Silver Lining

Martin Perez had a bizarre recurring dream—that he would find a mountain filled with riches. Stranger still, in his dream, the mountain resembled him in appearance. In 1940, Perez came across a mountain in the town of Mapimi, Mexico, whose outline looked very much like his own profile. Better still, the mountain had a rich vein of silver that would eventually make him millions!

Strike Four!

Major Summerford, an officer in the British Army during World War I, was struck three times by lightning: in 1918, in 1924, and in 1939. Four years after his death, lightning struck and destroyed his tombstone!

9

JUST PLAIN WEIRD

HOMING INSTINCT

If the Shoe Fits . . .

"I bought a shoe," Ruth Miller told her husband one day in 1995. "Only one?" he asked, sure that his wife was up to something. He was right. Ruth Miller had just purchased the Haines Shoe House in Hellam, Pennsylvania. It was built in 1948 by shoe store magnate Colonel Mahlon N. Haines. Miller gave tours of the five-story house until 2003, when she sold it to Carleen Farabaugh, who plans to keep up the tradition.

MADE TO SCALE

When glass is hard to come by, the Kamchatka people of Siberia sew translucent fish skins together to use in the windows of their homes.

Basket Case

Imagine how many people you could feed from a giant picnic basket! But look closer. What you see is not a basket but a seven-story building! It houses the corporate headquarters of the Longaberger Basket Company in Newark, Ohio. The handles alone weigh 150 tons. Synthetic plaster was used to sculpt the building's curved, basket-weave exterior. Then windows were placed between the spaces. The building sits on beautiful, parklike grounds—the perfect setting for the thousands of tourists who come to picnic there each year.

DOWN IN THE DUMPS

What do you do with tens of thousands of surplus carpet tiles? How about outdated parts from old car wrecks? If you're a member of the Rural Studio at Auburn University in Alabama, you won't throw them away. Instead, you'll use them to build a home, a chapel, or a library for people who are down on their luck. The Rural Studio is the inspiration of the late Samuel Mockbee, who believed architects have the power to change lives, along with the responsibility to lift spirits and shelter bodies.

Architecture students at the Rural Studio spend the school year living in Hale County, Alabama. Encouraged to let their imaginations run free, they work in teams to complete projects that will enhance the lives of the many poor people in the area. The challenge is to use worthless castoffs to save money while creating inviting one-of-a-kind structures. Students have built houses out of bales of hay, old tires, concrete rubble, colored bottles, and even old license plates.

Samuel Mockbee made his reputation building homes for the rich but gave up his private practice in order to use his gifts to create a better world. For his efforts, Mockbee received a MacArthur Fellowship, known as the "genius award," in 2002. Though he died of leukemia before he could use the $500,000 grant, students at the Rural Studio honor him by continuing his good work. Mockbee's legacy also lives on in the pride people of Hale County feel for their communities.

1. West Hollywood, California

Everything tastes better at Tail o' the Pup, an eatery that serves hot dogs and hamburgers. You can't miss it because the building is shaped like a giant frankfurter-filled hot dog roll. "Bun" appétit!

3. Mitchell, South Dakota

The Mitchell Corn Palace is covered from top to bottom with—you guessed it—corn! Every year, it gets a makeover, including brand-new murals. To create the pictures, it takes more than 3,000 bushels of corn in 11 different colors as well as about 40 tons of other grains and grasses!

2. Holbrook, Arizona

Listed in the National Register of Historic Places, Wigwam Village is quite an unusual roadside motel. Actually, the 14 units aren't wigwams at all, but rooms constructed in the shape of traditional Native American teepees.

PACIFIC OCEAN

MEXICO

4. Collinsville, Illinois

When the owners of Brooks Foods built a water tower for their catsup plant in 1947, they decided to make it look like a catsup bottle to promote their business. When the property was sold to a military supply company, the tower was scheduled for demolition. Folks in Collinsville, however, made a monumental effort to save the 170-foot-tall tower, raising $70,000 to restore it to its former glory.

CANADA

ATLANTIC OCEAN

6

UNITED STATES

4

5

6. Long Island, New York

In 1931, Martin and Jeule Maurer built a duck-shaped building on their duck farm in Riverhead. They hoped customers would be attracted to the Big Duck, which doubled as a store. It worked, and the store was a great success. Years later, the 20,000-pound, 20-foot-tall concrete duck was moved to its current site on Route 24 near Hampton Bays.

5. Lexington, Kentucky

Built in 1974, Bondurant's Pharmacy is shaped like a huge mortar and pestle, the tools pharmacists use to grind and mix medicine. You don't even have to get out of your car to get a prescription filled. You just drop it off at one window, then drive around to the other to pick it up.

ACCEPTING
MOST MEDICARE
DISCOUNT CARDS

BONDURANT'S

NASTY AND GROSS!

Frog Frenzy

It may not ever rain cats and dogs, but sometimes storms deliver more than mere rain, snow, or hail. History is full of reports of fish, jellyfish, snails, frogs, and even snakes falling from the sky. There's a written account of a storm of frogs that took place in about C.E. 200 in Macedonia, a region of ancient Greece. So many frogs fell on the roads, houses, and fields that people couldn't help but step on them as they escaped from the city. Squish!

Real Koala Kitsch

Collecting koala manure is turning out to be a fine way to make an easy buck in the small town of Gunnedah, Australia, which calls itself the "Koala Capital of the World." At the town's visitor center, tourists can buy Koala Kitsch, baggies of dried koala droppings. "I'm just glad we're not the elephant capital of the world," quipped tourist officer Chris Frend.

Thar She Blows!

After a whale died when it beached itself on the coast of Taiwan in January 2004, researchers hoisted the 60-ton carcass onto a truck to take it to the National Cheng Kung University in Tainan. It had almost reached its destination when gases from internal decay caused the whale to explode—all over the shops and cars on the busy street. The odor was so foul that residents and shopkeepers had to wear masks as they tried to clean up the mess. Luckily, from the marine biologists' point of view, enough of the whale was left for them to examine.

RIPLEY FILE: 10.28.02

Fatheads!
In place of liquid perfumes, the ancient Egyptians wore large cones of scented fat on their heads that slowly melted and dribbled all over their bodies.

DIAMONDS IN THE ROUGH

When a cow swallowed a bag containing 1,722 diamonds, its owner, Dilubhai Rajput, a diamond merchant in India, had to sift through piles of cow dung to retrieve them!

DOWN THE HATCH

Bug Bites

Have you ever eaten fried scorpions on shrimp toast? How about Shanhai mountain ants on shoestring potatoes? Over half the people in the world dine on some version of creepy-crawlies. David Gordon, author of *The Eat a Bug Cookbook*, is a big fan of bug cuisine. Barbecued grasshopper kabobs top his list for flavor and nutrition. Pound for pound, dried grasshoppers have as much protein as ground beef. The truth is, it's very likely you've already eaten a bug or two. For every 3.5 ounces of product, the Food and Drug Administration allows up to 60 insect fragments in chocolate, 30 fly eggs in tomato sauce, and 30 insect parts in peanut butter. *Crunch!*

WASTE NOT, WANT NOT

Gelatin is made from animal skins, hooves, and skeletons. It's used as a thickener for many types of foods, such as ice cream and cereal.

Pop Goes the Gravy

The makers of Turkey & Gravy Soda were having trouble keeping their new product on the shelves. Seattle-based Jones Soda Company was pleased to report that the flavor sold way beyond their wildest dreams. That's why in 2004, they offered a five-pack of soda consisting of Turkey & Gravy, Green Bean Casserole, Mashed Potato, Cranberry, and Fruitcake flavors—just in time for the holidays.

Vermin, Anyone?

A dinner given by Dinu Singh of Uttar Pradesh, India, was a huge success. Traditional favorites were served, including a rat buffet with mice meat kabobs. The rodents, caught in the hills of Bundelkhand, are also roasted, pureed, and made into soups. Although the practice of eating mice and rats began at a time when poverty was widespread, now well-to-do city dwellers celebrate their success by serving these old-fashioned traditional dishes to remind them of their heritage.

RIPLEY FILE: 10.15.04

Freaky Fry-days! For his documentary film *Supersize Me*, director Morgan Spurlock ate nothing but fast food for breakfast, lunch, and dinner over the course of 30 days.

FUN-EMPLOYMENT

THE DAILY GRIND!

The people responsible for grinding Dijon mustard were often given bonuses when fumes from the vats made them cry on the job.

Stinko-saurus

Frank Knight of Great Britain specializes in creating themed aromas. Some of the scents concocted in his lab are pleasantly designed to get customers to linger in a particular area of a store. Others are, well, funkier. Knight consulted with a paleontologist when he was asked to design a scent for London's Natural History Museum. The assignment? To recreate the breath of a Tyrannosaurus rex. Knight learned from the experts that this dinosaur would have had open wounds from fighting and rancid hunks of meat between its teeth. The scent ended up being so disgusting that he was asked to tone it down!

Cutting-Edge Work

To do her job, all Yana Rodianova had to do is stand perfectly still. Sound easy? It would be if circus performer Jayde Hanson were not hurling knives at the wall behind her. More than a million TV viewers were watching the day Hanson nicked Rodianova while trying to throw 60 knives in one minute. In 11 years of knife-throwing, Hanson has only hit his assistants five times, but Rodianova isn't taking any more chances. She has decided to look for a different line of work, and is currently perfecting her hula-hoop act. Rodianova and Hanson are still partners, though, because the two have since become husband and wife!

RIPLEY FILE: 9.7.52

Hot job market! Emperor Akbar (1542–1602) of India forced every candidate for high office to compete with him in a game of night polo—using balls of fire made from slow-burning wood.

Elf-ology

Magnus Skarphedinsson of Reykjavik, Iceland, is an elf historian and headmaster of the Icelandic Elf School, which has issued more than 4,000 diplomas in elf studies. According to Skarphedinsson, more than half the population of Iceland believes in elves, gnomes, and other such creatures.

WHEEL LIFE

Big Wheels!

Fans of monster truck events are thrilled by the sight of muscle trucks. Loud, huge, and powerful, these trucks are monsters, indeed! One truck in the Bigfoot series sports Firestone Tundra tires, each weighing 2,400 pounds. The tires are tall, too! Sitting high on their 10-foot-tall wheels, the drivers rev their engines to a deafening roar and race the trucks up a monster ramp. Up through the air they sail. Then down they come with a heavy thud, crushing the rows of cars below like so many soda cans. Crunch!

Easy Rider

The Tombstone Hearse Company, with locations in four states, offers an alternative to a plain old Cadillac or Lincoln hearse. Combining old-fashioned glass-sided hearses and converted Harley Davidson motorcycles, the company will not only carry the deceased to the cemetery but also take him or her on a last ride past a favorite place or along a favorite road.

In High Gear

Retired engineer Jim Reinders was looking for something to do. Why not create a monument? he thought. Since there were no large stones in western Nebraska, he decided to work with what the state had a lot of—old cars. The result is Carhenge, a towering work made up of 39 cars. Each year, more than 82,000 tourists visit the monument on Highway 87 in Alliance, even though it's 90 miles away from the nearest freeway.

Out of steam! On September 18, 1830, the steam locomotive Tom Thumb, invented by Peter Cooper in Baltimore, Maryland, raced a horse-drawn carriage—and lost!

ALL ABOARD!

The town of Lakewood, Australia, a community in the heart of a lumber and gold mining region, has its homes, shops, post office, and police station mounted on railroad cars.

JOY RIDES

Smile!

Harrod Blank's camera van is a metal mosaic of sophisticated design. A fully functional vehicle, the van has more than 2,000 cameras attached to it. The cameras, including ten video cameras, are operated by shutter buttons on the driver's side of the dashboard. On the passenger side, 13 color monitors display the photographic results. So if you happen to see the camera van in your neck of the woods, don't forget to say cheese!

RIPLEY FILE: 10.18.04

Long hauler! Limousine business owners Bobby Sims and Sheila Moon rent out a custom truck limo that is 40 feet long, weighs almost 9,000 pounds, and gets a whopping five miles to the gallon.

120

Radical Roadster

Many people might argue that the second most important character in the James Bond movies is his car. When it comes to bells and whistles, the 1963 silver Aston Martin DB5 used in the movie *Goldfinger* is without equal. Special features include a license plate with revolving numbers for every country, a passenger ejector seat, bulletproof windows, mounted machine guns, an oil slick producer, and retractable tire-shredders. No wonder James Bond always comes out of his scrapes unscathed!

Good Car-ma

Most celebrities like to move about freely without worrying about the paparazzi or autograph seekers. That's why so many opt for ordinary-looking vehicles—ordinary on the outside, that is. Unassuming Chevy Suburbans and Ford Excursions get souped-up engines and passenger areas with offices fitted out with top-of-the-line computers, TVs, stereos, and telephones. Barbra Streisand's roadster has been stretched to accommodate everything from a jacuzzi to a toilet!

FAST FORWARD

Due to its extremely lightweight body and powerful engine, the world's fastest car, the Swedish Koenigsegg CCR, reaches a speed of 389 miles per hour and covers a quarter mile in just ten seconds!

EXTRA! EXTRA!

Forward Thinking

In 2003, when Harpreet Devi of Bhatinda, India, had car trouble, he came up with a unique solution. Stuck in reverse with 35 miles left to go to reach home, Devi decided to drive backward! Now he and his wife, Krishna, drive everywhere in reverse at speeds of up to 25 miles per hour—even in heavy traffic. The "reverse couple," as they are called locally, have no plans to change their driving style any time soon!

Miles to Go

In the early 1930s, Charles Miller of Portland, Oregon, saved a whole lot of money on hotel bills. Miller lived in a clapboard house perched atop his six-foot-long vehicle for more than two years and toured the country in it nine times. The car had more than 200,000 miles on it when he purchased it. Miller added 200,000 more!

Wear a Helmet!

What do you do with a car that's too old to be reliable? You could take it to a demolition derby like the one held at the Kitsap County Fairgrounds in Bremerton, Washington. Contestants strip their old cars of dangerous materials and reinforce them so they can take a licking. Once the race begins, the sound of crunching metal and shattering headlights fills the air. Drivers drop out of the competition when their cars will no longer move. The last car still running is the winner. Crash!

Dream House

The Nightcap House was built around the turn of the 20th century, by a man who patterned his home after the hat a governor of the French colony of New Caledonia wore to bed every night—complete with a tassel on top!

Star Struck

Founded in 1593, the town of Palmanova, Italy, was designed so that, viewed from above, it would resemble a nine-pointed star.

Making a Splash

For those who can't afford the real thing, there's a new fragrance for men on the market. Called Hummer, the cologne comes in a bottle shaped like the distinctive grille of the Hummer H2. So if you can't own a Hummer, smelling like one might just be the next best thing.

Milk Dud

In 2004, a retired man was hit by a milk truck driven by Monty, a black Labrador retriever. The dog, who belongs to the milkman, usually sits in the back of the truck and waits patiently for his master to return after delivering each order. On this day, however, Monty jumped into the driver's seat and stepped on the gas while the milkman was making a delivery. The man he hit had a grazed knee, and Monty had a slightly injured paw. Both made a speedy recovery.

Home Economics

In the late 1700s, the owners of the castle of Verres, Italy, ruined it on purpose by removing the roof. Why? Buildings without roofs were not taxable.

Auto-Plane

A limousine company in Mexico uses a converted Boeing 727 passenger plane to carry people down the highway at speeds of up to 125 miles per hour.

10

ODDS AND ENDS

GOOFY GARB

Doggy Duds

Victoria Pettigrew of VIP Fibers Inc. really knows how to put on the dog—literally. She's actually in the business of spinning dog hair into beautiful yarn. She then crochets the yarn into one-of-kind sweaters, shawls, coats, mittens, and other items for her customers to wear. Grieving dog owners often send her their late pets' fur to be made into an article of clothing, so that they will always have a warm reminder of their dearly departed companion.

WARM HANDS, WARM HEARTS

Terence David King of Great Britain has invented gloves that fit two people at once so that couples can stay nice and warm while holding hands.

Corn Job

In 1947, Virginia Winn of Mercedes, Texas, cobbled together 60,000 grains of corn to decorate an evening dress. The completed garment weighed 40 pounds!

Show me the money! In the 1700s, the attire American women of the South wore to church determined how much money their husbands were required to put into the church collection plate. The more elegant the clothing, the more money required.

Bright Idea

Fashion designer Janet Hansen of San Diego, California, has always been turned on by design and technology. She trained for a career in engineering and eventually combined her two major interests, fashion and technology, to form her own company called Enlighted Designs, Inc. Each of Hansen's fashions has a built-in light show that can last for up to ten hours. Sewn into a seam in each battery-powered article of clothing is a computer chip that stores all of the light pattern information for hours of turned-on fun.

AWESOME!

Wizard of Words

Twelve-year-old Ben Buchanan, who lives near Dallas, Texas, would like to be a famous author and illustrator when he grows up. The fact that he has dyslexia is not about to hold him back. In fact, young Ben has already made a good start: He's had two books published. *My Year with Harry Potter* describes what it's like to have dyslexia and how the Harry Potter books inspired him to conquer his reading disability. *Journey to Gameland: How to Make a Board Game from Your Favorite Children's Book* is based on Ben's experience inventing his own Harry Potter game.

The Write Stuff

Who says you have to wait until you're an adult to write your first novel? Romanian-born Flavia Bujor of Paris, France, was age 12 when she started *The Prophecy of the Stones*, and 14 when it was published. It's about a young girl in the hospital, who imagines another world where three young women work together to save their land with the help of some magic stones. Published in France, Italy, Germany, and the United States, it is well on its way to becoming a bestseller.

STREET SMARTS

Liz Murray's story is so amazing that Hollywood made a TV movie about her life, starring Thora Birch. And no wonder. Charles Dickens himself couldn't have made up a more compelling story. Born to drug-addicted parents, Murray lived in a filthy, rat-infested apartment in South Bronx, New York. To keep from going hungry, she found a job bagging groceries when she was just eight years old. She stayed home from school to avoid being teased by kids who made fun of her appearance. Nonetheless, Murray got an education by reading every book she could get her hands on at the library, including encyclopedias.

Murray was left homeless at age 15, when her mother was hospitalized with AIDS and died a year later. At the cemetery, reality dawned on Murray. She, alone, was responsible for her life. *What if I woke up and every single day, I did everything within my ability to change my life?* Murray asked herself. She vowed her life would not go to waste as her mother's had.

Murray kept her word. She enrolled in high school, doubling up on her courses and completing one full year per semester. Each day, she stayed at school until the janitor locked the doors. During the night, she rode the subway back and forth until morning, then started the routine all over again. Murray finished high school in just two years—and graduated second in her class. She won a full scholarship from *The New York Times* and in 2000, was accepted into Harvard, majoring in film and literature. In 2003, she transferred to Columbia University. Today, Murray accepts speaking engagements at inner-city high schools, where she serves as an inspiration to other students who have no one in their lives to encourage them.

ON THE BALL

In 2003, Gabriela Ferreira became the newest soccer commentator on the biggest radio station in Sao Paulo, Brazil. Not bad for a ten-year-old girl!

ODDBALL ART

Last Paper Bag

In 1985, Anton Schiavone of Bangor, Pennsylvania, created a life-sized replica of Leonardo Da Vinci's *Last Supper* out of brown-paper grocery bags that his neighbors helped him collect from the local supermarket.

RIPLEY FILE:
4.5.04

Miniature marvels! A tiny art gallery in Buenos Aires, Argentina, has a one-foot-high ceiling. Patrons must put their heads through a hole to see the 27 miniature paintings and sculptures on exhibit.

Chew on This!

Franz Spohn, professor of art at Edinboro University in Pennsylvania, creates one-of-a-kind masterpieces out of gumballs. He achieves his creations by filling plastic tubes with 130 gumballs at a time so that he can create huge murals. He also specializes in what he calls "sweet pointillism," mosaics that are made with thousands of brightly colored candy sprinkles.

Shooting the Works

In the 1930s, Ernie and Dot Lind were known for the bullet-hole art they created by shooting at canvases rather than painting them.

Wood You Believe?

Livio de Marchi of Venice, Italy, is a sculptor whose major medium is wood. His creations, however, range from shirts, jackets, and ties to life-sized floating cars. He even creates houses made out of wood blocks that look like books. Inside, everything is wood, from the armchairs to the clothes that hang in the closets to the curtains and bed linens!

WHAT A PILL!

When it comes to using unusual materials, artist Tom Friedman is king! In 1994, he carved a self-portrait out of a single aspirin and used his own hair to sculpt a tarantula!

BODY OF ART

RIPLEY FILE: 6.14.72

Heads and tails! Young Aborigines of Central Australia weave the hairs of their beard around the curved tail of a thalgoo—an Australian mammal.

Bone-ified!

In the 1700s, Josiah Spode discovered that adding finely ground cow bones to clay gave his china a beautiful translucent quality. Today, many companies make bone china, but it took artist Charles Krafft of Seattle, Washington, to come up with the idea of Spone china—pieces incorporating the ashes from cremated human bones. Krafft's commemorative pieces can be anything from a plate to a shovel to an infantry helmet. Among his most memorable creations, however, is a Spone bulldog that incorporates the remains of veterinarian Robert Thornberry.

THE HUMAN 3

Stun Gun

Visitors to an art show in Amsterdam, the Netherlands, were shocked to discover the material that was used to create one of the exhibits was the artist's own skin! Dutch artist Joanneke Meester had an eight-inch-long piece of her skin surgically removed. After stretching the skin, she used it to cover a plastic and fiber pistol mold.

Jewelry to Die For

Jewelry designer Hilda Marshall, also known as Columbine, makes designer jewelry from human bones—delicate bracelets from fingers and chunkier pieces from larger bones. She got the idea for her macabre collection when a friend in medical school gave her a bag of bones that had become separated from their skeletons. Now she gets her bones from medical schools and universities that have decided to replace their human skeletons with more uniform plastic models.

Going Batty

Mexican artist Enrico Angelis Ramos creates paintings on dead animals, such as his recent collection of paintings on the outstretched wings of bats. Though it takes the talented Ramos mere minutes to complete his portraits of famous people, it takes him hours to catch his canvases!

SNAPPY ACCESSORIES!

Kathy Richard of Abbeville, Louisiana, creates jewelry out of alligator bones and teeth.

WILD RIDES

Thrills and Chills

Ohio's Cedar Point Amusement Park is home to Top Thrill Dragster, the world's fastest—and tallest—roller coaster. Riders sit in cars that look just like drag racers. Due to Top Thrill's powerful hydraulic launch system, passengers reach the incredible speed of 120 miles per hour in mere seconds, and the 420-foot-tall top of the coaster in just a few seconds more. As if that weren't enough, Top Thrill has vertical twists and turns and, in one spot, a vertical 400-foot-drop!

Having a Blast!

Ever wonder what it feels like to get shot out of a volcano? You can find out at King's Dominion amusement park in Doswell, Virginia. The thrills start right away for passengers on The Volcano. Seated in a ski lift–style chair, they are literally left hanging, as they dangle from a steel track high above the ground. More than a roller coaster, the 155-foot-tall ride actually blasts its riders through the top of a "volcano" at a speed of 70 miles per hour!

Step Right Up!

At the Circus Circus Casino in Las Vegas, Nevada, you can ride the Canyon Blaster no matter what the weather is outside. A huge pink dome and air-conditioning protect riders from extremes in temperature.

A FLYING LEAP

At the A. J. Hackett Bungee Jump in Las Vegas, Nevada, you can leap from a height of 171.5 feet—all you have to do is trust the rubber cord to keep you from hitting the ground!

WACKY STUFF

The Beet Goes On

Austrian musicians in the Vienna Vegetable Orchestra get paid to play with their food. Founder Jörg Piringer plays a reed instrument called a gurkaphon, which is made from a hollowed-out cucumber, green pepper, and carrot. Other "Veggies" play carrot flutes, leek violins, radish marimbas, and eggplant cymbals. After each concert, a chef appears to make vegetable soup from the instruments—which becomes an après concert treat for musicians and audience alike.

NO FUSS, NO MUSS

Instead of washing dishes, get dinnerware made from wheat by a company in Taiwan and just eat your plate along with your meal.

Hung Out to Dry

Eduardo Segura and Andrés Diaz, two entrepreneurs from Spain, have created Lavakan, an automatic pet washing machine. Just stick your four-legged friend inside the machine, pick the best wash cycle for your pet's size, then wait 20 minutes for your pet laundry to be done. Diaz claims it's just like giving your pet a water massage. The price? That's the catch. Lavakan costs $20,000, so only vets and grooming businesses are buying them—but don't worry: Segura and Diaz are working on a personal pet washing machine that will be less costly. Stay tuned.

RIPLEY FILE: 3.18.97

Well armed! British Telecom has developed a portable office consisting of a display screen, a microprocessor keypad, and a mobile phone that all attach to a person's arm.

Golden Opportunity

A solid gold soccer ball, created to commemorate Japan's second straight Asian Cup, could have been yours had you been at Tokyo's Mitsukoshi department store at the right time on August 9, 2004. Oh, yes, you would have needed a nice chunk of change to seal the deal—the equivalent of $182,000 to be exact.

EXTRA! EXTRA!

Clip Art

California artist Tim Hawkinson frequently makes his sculptures using parts of his own body, including a two-inch-tall piece called *Bird* that was made entirely from his own fingernails.

Con Artist

If it weren't for the talent of forensic artist Lois Gibson, it's likely that more than 700 criminal cases in Texas would have gone unsolved. Gibson's unique ability to translate a victim's memory of his or her attacker into an uncanny likeness of the criminal have made her an invaluable asset to police.

Sock It to Me!

Researchers at the University of California at Davis have developed socks that stay fresh and odorless even after they've been worn for several days.

Frozen Tidal Wave

Using the usual ingredients, Jan van de Berg of Katwijk aan den Rijn, the Netherlands, made a giant ice pop that weighed 20,020 pounds.

What a Load!

On January 26, 2004, visitors to a London art gallery were astonished to see artist Gavin Turk's latest work. Called *Pile*, this bronze casting of a huge, bulging garbage bag had a price tag the equivalent of $136,000.

Sticking with It

Robert McDonald of Emmeloord, the Netherlands, built a boat out of 370,000 lollipop sticks. It was about ten feet long and eight feet wide. Encouraged by the fact that he actually stayed afloat in it for 19 minutes, McDonald now plans to build an exact replica of a Viking ship. All he needs are 15 million sticks. That's a lot of lollipops!

N-ice Job

As a starving artist in Harlem, New York, David Hammons sold snowballs for whatever he could get. These days, however, Hammons commands up to $100,000 for a single artwork!

C-shirts

The Fuji Spinning Company in Japan has developed a brand-new way to take vitamins—all you have to do is wear their T-shirts, which are made with a fiber that contains provitamin. This chemical turns into Vitamin C as soon as it comes into contact with your skin!

Slick!

Sled enthusiasts don't need to lug along a sled when they wear this invention—pants with sleds built into them. They're made by inserting a sheet of tin into the pants and sealing it with wax.

INDEX

INDEX

PHOTO CREDITS

Ripley Entertainment Inc. and the editors of this book wish to thank the following photographers, agents, and other individuals for permission to use and reprint the following photographs in this book. Any photographs included in this book that are not acknowledged below are property of the Ripley Archives. Great effort has been made to obtain permission from the owners of all materials included in this book. Any errors that may have been made are unintentional and will gladly be corrected in future printings if notice is sent to Ripley Entertainment Inc., 5728 Major Boulevard, Orlando, Florida 32819.

COVER: Lizardman—Allen Falkner; Egyptian Mummy—Tom McHugh/Photo Researchers, Inc.; Vegetarian Festival—AP Photo/David Longstreath; Image—AP Photo/Jay Crawford; Bigfoot 5–AP Photo/Paul Warner

TITLE PAGE: Zamoratte—Newscom/Oliver Berg

TOC: Katzen and ThEnigma—The Human Marvels; Rico—Reuters/Manuela Hartling

INTRODUCTION: 5 Lizardman—Allen Falkner; **5** Camera Van—Harrod Blank

CHAPTER 1: 9, 13 El Colacho—AP Photo/Israel Lopez Murillo; **10** Pushkar Camel Fair—PictureQuest/Dave Bartruff; **11** Toad, **19** Panda, **21** Pizza—Ablestock; **11** Asiatic Black Bear, **16** Hermit Crab—CORBIS; **12** Bun Festival Parade—AP Photo/Vincent Yu; **12** Break-dancer—Newscom/Getty Images; **14** Bonvicini and Mirrored Toilet—Newscom/Andy Butterton; **14** Garment-covered Furniture—Janet Morton; **15** Outhouse Race–AP Photo/Bill Moffitt; **16** Crab Beauty Contest—AP Photo/Mary Godleski; **16** Zorb—www.zorb.com; **17** Red-tailed Hawk—Beth Jackson/Fish & Wildlife Service; **17** Pale Male Fledgling—AP Photo/Adam Rountree; **18** Terra-cotta Warriors—AP Photo/Neal Ulevich; **20** Sturgeon—Duane Raver/Fish & Wildlife Service

CHAPTER 2: 23, 30: X-ray—PictureQuest; **24** Intestinal Bacteria—SPL/Photo Researchers, Inc.; **24** Grossology Exhibit—photo courtesy of Advanced Animations LLC, the exhibit's developer and producer. Grossology is a registered trademark of Penguin Putnam Inc. For more information on the exhibit, please visit www.grossologytour.com; **25** Scabies Mite—Eye of Science/Photo Researchers, Inc.; **26** Trepanned Skulls, **26** George Washington—Library of Congress; **26** Egyptian Mummy—Tom McHugh/Photo Researchers, Inc.; **26** DNA—Alfred Pasieka/Photo Researchers, Inc.; **26** Stethoscope, **28** Airplane—Ablestock; **27** Barber-Surgeon–Art Resource; **27** Gall Bladder Surgery—Newscom; **28** Nicolelis and Monkey—AP Photo/Jim Wallace; **28** Spirit Seeker Sculpture—Courtesy of Ivan Schlutz; **29** Wain Cat Painting—Art Resource; **29** Wain Abstract Painting/The Bethlem Art and History Collections Trust; **31** Hand, Rubber Hand—L. C. Casterline; **31** Girl with Chocolate, **33** Mouse—CORBIS

CHAPTER 3: 35, 41 Recycled Fashion—AP Photo/Craig Houtz; **36** Titan Arum—AP Photo/Jerome T. Nakagawa; **37** Fly on Sundew—PictureQuest; **37** Indian Banyan Tree—Beatrice Neff/Photo Researchers, Inc.; **38** Rhinoceros—Digital Vision; **38** Thermal Processing—AP Photo/Mark Stehle; **39** Dr. Zhang—AP Photo/Tom Roberts; **39** Pig, **40** Rooster—Digital Vision; **40** Windhexe—Courtesy of Vortex Dehydration Technology; **41** Corn "Plastic"—AP Photo/Nati Harnik; **42** Asian Honeybees—Scott Camazine/Photo Researchers, Inc.; **42** Hailstone—AP Photo/Steve Swazo; **43** Tornado Destruction—AP Photo/Mark Elias;

44 Lightbulb, **45** Maggots—Ablestock

CHAPTER 4: 47, 52 Cathie Jung—Cathie Jung; **48** Robert Forster—AP Photo/Las Cruces Sun News/Norm Dettlatt; **48** Eyeball Jewelry—Newscom/Getty Images/Michel Porro; **49** Joanna Vaughn—Reuters/HO; **50** Masai Warriors, **50** Maori Chief—Library of Congress; **50** Mangbetu Woman—Leon Poirier and George Specht/Eliot Elisofon Photographic Archives, National Museum of African Art/Smithsonian Institution; **51** Vegetarian Festival—AP Photo/David Longstreath; **53** Katzen and ThEnigma—The Human Marvels; **53** Julia Gnuse—AP Photo/David J. Phillip; **54** Leonid Stadnik—AP Photo/Efrem Lukatsky; **54** Konishiki and Iijima—AP Photo/Chiaki Tsukumo; **55** Tran Van Hay—AP Photo/Thanh Nien

CHAPTER 5: 59, 68 Circus Act—AP Photo/Lionel Cironneau; **60** Bufa—Reuters; **60** Mary-Kate and Ashley—AP Photo/John Dunham; **61** Image—AP Photo/Jay Crawford; **62** Cow, **70** Prairie Dog—Ablestock; **62** Leopard, **67** Starfish—Corel; **63** Cat and Skunk—Newscom; **63** Dog and Fawn—Newscom/Wolfgang Kluge; **64** Elephants—PictureQuest; **65** Rico—Reuters/Manuela Hartling; **65** Crow Using Tool—Behavioural Ecology Research Group, Oxford University; **66** Isopod—1983 Brusca, R. C. and M. R. Gilligan/Tongue replacement in a marine fish (Lutjanas guttatus) by a parasitic isopod (Crustacea: Isopoda) Copeia 3: 813-816; **66** Crab with Parasite—USGS.gov/Todd Huspeni; **67** Herring—Getty Images/Ken Usami; **69** Sirull and Brutus—Tom Sanders; **69** Twiggy—Newscom/Manny Millan/SI/Icon SMI; **71** Hamster—Photodisc Green

CHAPTER 6: 73, 78 Zamoratte—Newscom/Oliver Berg; **74** Brush-turkey—Visuals Unlimited/Theo Allofs; **74** Bear—CORBIS; **75** Hamilton—AP Photo/Ronen Zilberman; **76** Boa—Getty Images/Ryan McVay; **76** Extension Cord, **76** Cat, **80** Cat—Ablestock; **77** Dick—AP Photo/Tim Roske; **78** Mejia, X-Ray—AP Photo/Damian Dovarganes; **79** Novotny—AP Photo/Jamie Piontkowski; **80** Airplane—Reuters/POOL/Ed Wray; **81** Carp—Eric Engbretson/Fish & Wildlife Service

CHAPTER 7: 83, 86 Ghost King—AP Photo/Vincent Yu; **84** Stuffed Bird—Courtesy of A Case of Curiosities; **84** Archer and Tasmanian Tiger—Reuters/DG; **85** Gurnee—Shmuel Thaler/Santa Cruz Sentinel; **87** Hampton Court Ghost—AP Photo/Hampton Court Palace; **87** Queen Mary—Newscom/Alan Solomon; **88** Headrick Memorial Disc—Courtesy of Disc Golf Association, Inc.; **88** Thumbie—Courtesy of www.thumbies.com; **89** Frozen Dead Guy Days—Barbara Lawlor; **90** Ötzi—Newscom/AFP Photo; **90** Bog Mummy and Reconstruction—Courtesy of Drents Museum, Assen, the Netherlands; **91** Chinese Mummy—AP Photo/Dolkun Kamberi; **91** Anasazi Mummy—CORBIS/Dewitt Jones; **92** Trumpet, **93** Cocktails—Ablestock

CHAPTER 8: 95, 98 Red-bellied Black Snake—PictureQuest; **96** Wat Phra Kaeo—CORBIS; **97** Revolutionary War Re-enactment—Getty Images; **97** Quarters, **98** Old Money, **101** Money—Iram Khandwala; **98** Termites—AP Photo/Victor R. Caivano; **99** Hartge Rescue—AP Photo/The Star Democrat/Roxane Doster Watts; **99** Crystal Ball—Ablestock; **100** Billy D'Onofrio—AP Photo/New-Times/Silas Crews; **101** Airplane—Getty Images/Jay Brousseau; **101** McDonald's Sign—Atif Toor; **102** Old Men—Getty Images; **102** Bottle with Message—Getty Images/Steve Cole; **103** Rabi and Scott—Newscom/Matt Campbell; **104** Football, **104** Old Camera—Ablestock; **105** Ants—Corel

CHAPTER 9: 107, 118 Bigfoot 5—AP Photo/Paul Warner; **108** Shoe House—AP Photo/Joseph Kaczmarek; **108** Longaberger Headquarters—Newscom; **109** Rural Studio (Shiles)—Timothy Hursley; **109** Rural Studio—AP Photo/Michael E. Palmer; **110** Tail o' the Pup—Newscom/Spencer Grant; **110** Mitchell Corn Palace—AP Photo/Doug Dreyer; **110** Wigwam Village—AP Photo/Alisa Blackwood; **111** Brooks Foods Tower—Courtesy of www.catsupbottle.com; **111** Bondurant Pharmacy—Courtesy of Bondurant Pharmacy & BruWare LLC; **111** Big Duck—Courtesy of Suffolk County Department of Parks; **112** Frogs, **112** Cloudy Sky—Ablestock; **112** Koala—Newscom/Torsten Blackwood; **113** Sperm Whale—Newscom/STR; **114** Grasshopper Kabobs—Scott Stenjem; **114** Gordon—AP Photo/Wong Maye-e; **115** Jones Soda—AP Photo/Ted S. Warren; **115** Rat—PictureQuest; **116** Tyrannosaurus rex—Newscom/BWP Media; **117** Hanson and Rodianova—Newscom/Chris Ison; **117** Elf—Getty Images/David Perry; **118** Motorcycle Hearse—Courtesy of The Tombstone Hearse Company; **119** Carhenge—AP Photo/David Zalubowski; **120** Camera Van—Harrod Blank; **121** Bond's Aston Martin—Newscom/KRT; **121** SUV Limousine—AP Photo/Charlie Riedel; **123** Labrador Retriever—L. C. Casterline

CHAPTER 10: 125, 134 Top Thrill Dragster—AP Photo/Sandusky Register/Daniel Miller; **126** Dog-hair Sweater—Courtesy of www.vip-fibers.com; **126** Dog, **126** Corn Kernels, **127** Lightbulb, **129** Subway, **139** Lollipops—Ablestock; **127** Light-up Coat—Courtesy of Janet Hansen of Enlighted.com; **128** Ben Buchanan's Books—Newscom/MBR; **128** Flavia Bujor—AP Photo/Michel Euler; **130** Franz Spohn—Courtesy of Franz Spohn; **132** Charles Krafft—AP Photo/Ted S. Warren; **133** Skin Gun—Newscom/AFP Photo/Continental, **133** Bone Jewelry—Courtesy of Sunspot Designs; **134** The Volcano—Paramount's King's Dominion; **135** Canyon Blaster—Joe Schwartz; **136** Vienna Vegetable Orchestra—Newscom/Mathias Friedrich; **137** Lavakan—Courtesy of Lavakan; **137** Gold Soccer Ball—Newscom/Toru Yamanaka; **138** Clipping Nails—L. C. Casterline